I hope the book gives you many
hours of interest.

FALLING TO PIECES

FALLING TO PIECES

*Making sense of self-deception
and the divided mind*

Jeremy Havardi

Artwork by Daniel Havardi

The Book Guild Ltd
Sussex, England

First published in Great Britain in 2004 by
The Book Guild Ltd
25 High Street
Lewes, East Sussex
BN7 2LU

Typesetting in Times by
Keyboard Services, Luton, Bedfordshire

Printed in Great Britain by
CPI Bath

A catalogue record for this book is available from
The British Library

ISBN 1 85776 835 3

*To Ben   Doreen, Daniel, Richard, Nissim
and Edith*

Contents

Contents

Acknowledgements

According to Paul Cinguine, when one reads a book, one is a slave to the author's mind. I hope, in this instance, that the reader's temporary enslavement will not prove to be completely futile. Self-deception is an interesting topic and this book aims to present a clear picture of the phenomenon. If it provides this clarification, I will have achieved at least a small success.

This book started out as a dissertation submitted for an MPhil degree for King's College, University of London. It has been expanded with the addition of a final chapter on irrationality, and a lengthy discussion on deception in the first chapter. While modifications have been made to the original text, essentially the ideas have altered very little since the work was successfully submitted for the degree some five years ago. I would like to thank the tutors at King's for their encouragement while this was being written. In particular, I must thank Jim Hopkins, who fiercely cast a critical eye on what I had written. Without his help and suggestions this work would have taken much longer to complete. I also owe a heavy debt to the work of Donald Davidson. His philosophy of mind has influenced my way of thinking in many respects, and this will become clear in my work.

I would like to thank my parents and family for their

Acknowledgements

According to Paul Gauguin, when one reads a book, one is a slave to the author's mind. I hope, in this instance, that the reader's temporary enslavement will not prove to be completely futile. Self-deception is an interesting topic and this book aims to present a clear picture of the phenomenon. If it provides this clarification, I will have achieved at least a small success.

This book started out as a dissertation submitted for an MPhil degree for King's College, University of London. It has been expanded with the addition of a final chapter on irrationality and a lengthy discussion on deception in the first chapter. While modifications have been made to the original text, essentially the ideas have altered very little since the work was successfully submitted for the degree some five years ago. I would like to thank the tutors at King's for their encouragement while this was being written. In particular, I must thank Jim Hopkins, who tirelessly cast a critical eye on what I had written. Without his help and suggestions, this work would have taken much longer to complete. I also owe a heavy debt to the work of Donald Davidson. His philosophy of mind has influenced my way of thinking in many respects and this will become clear in my work.

I would like to thank my parents and family for their

constant support and, in particular, my mother for her valiant efforts at proofreading and the corrections she suggested. I finally owe a debt of gratitude to my copy editor, Julian Beecroft. His suggestions and comments proved invaluable.

Jeremy Havardi,
London 2003

The author and publishers wish to thank the following for their kind permission to reproduce material in this book: *Human Inference: Strategies and Shortcomings of Social Judgement* by Nisbet/Ross, © Reprinted by permission of Pearson Education, Inc., Upper Saddle River, NJ. Sigmund Freud © Copyrights, The Institute of Psychoanalysis and The Hogarth Press for permission to quote from *The Standard Edition Of The Complete Psychological Works Of Sigmund Freud* translated and edited by James Strachey. Reprinted by permission of The Random House Group Limited. *Self-Deception and Self-Understanding: New Essays in Philosophy and Psychology*, by Mike W Martin, published by the University Press of Kansas © 1985. www.kansaspress.ku.edu. Used by permission of the publisher. *The Varnished Truth* by D Nyberg (1993), © Reprinted by permission of the University of Chicago Press. *Perspectives of Self-Deception* by Brian McLaughlin and Amelie Rorty, Copyright © 1988 The Regents of the University of California, reprinted by permission of the University of California Press. *Philosophical Essays on Freud* by J Hopkins and R Wollheim, 1982, reprinted by permission of Cambridge University Press. *Seeing Through Self-Deception* by A Barnes, 1997, reprinted by permission of Cambridge University Press. *Irrationality and the Philosophy of Psychoanalysis* by S Gardiner, 1993, reprinted by permission of Cambridge University Press.

Preface

Self-deception is something entirely familiar to us in everyday life. We readily see our loved ones and friends fooling themselves when we wish they could only see the world with objectivity and lucidity. We can discern self-deception in the clever disguises of alcoholics and gamblers who dive in denial despite their manifestly harmful addictions. We acknowledge the blindness of love but ignore the failures in our own relationships. Though we may not always have the right words to describe what we see, there seems little doubt that self-deception is a common and widespread form of irrationality.

Recent history, in particular the last world war, is replete with cases of apparent self-deception. Hermann Goering's reaction to news that an allied fighter had been shot down over Germany is a classic exercise in wishful myopia. Goering could not bring himself to accept that an American plane had been shot down over Aachen, and that the Allies therefore had combat aircraft capable of flying long-range missions over his country. His response was that the report was impossible and he officially denied that there was any truth in the idea.

Stalin was responsible for another catastrophic political misjudgement by consistently refusing to believe that Nazi Germany would attack his country. The consequences of

Preface

Self-deception is something entirely familiar to us in everyday life. We readily see our loved ones and friends 'fooling themselves' when we wish they could only see the world with objectivity and lucidity. We can discern self-deception in the clever disguises of alcoholics and gamblers who live in denial despite their manifestly harmful addictions. We acknowledge the blindness of love but ignore the failures in our own relationships. Though we may not always have the right words to describe what we see, there seems little doubt that self-deception is a common and widespread form of irrationality.

Recent history, in particular the last world war, is replete with cases of apparent self-deception. Hermann Goering's reaction to news that an allied fighter had been shot down over Germany is a classic exercise in wilful myopia. Goering could not bring himself to accept that an American plane had been shot down over Aachen, and that the Allies therefore had combat aircraft capable of flying long-range missions over his country. His response was that the report was impossible and he officially denied that there was any truth in the idea.

Stalin was responsible for another catastrophic political misjudgement by consistently refusing to believe that Nazi Germany would attack his country. The consequences of this dogmatic stance were to make Russia more vulnerable to attack, leading to an appalling civilian casualty rate. In the four months prior to invasion, Stalin received dozens of reports of the impending Operation Barbarossa from numerous sources, among them Churchill and the German ambassador in Russia, Count von der Schulenberg. Stalin ignored all these warnings, as did the head of the NKVD, Lavrenti Beria. Indeed, Beria stated that NKVD officials who sent reports of German attack plans ought to be ground into 'labour camp dust'. German forces crossed into Russian territory in June 1941 at the start of Operation Barbarossa. When news reached Moscow on the day of the German invasion, the official response in Moscow was that the messenger was 'insane'. If it is the case that this overwhelmingly strong information was deliberately ignored in order to allay anxieties, we have a clear candidate for self-deception. Knowing the potentially catastrophic losses that a German invasion would entail, with the resultant admission of failure, wilful denial of evidence seems entirely understandable. It may also be that this behaviour was transferred from leader to subordinates, demonstrating the capacity for shared irrational responses to conflict situations.

In this context, the Nazi-Soviet non-aggression pact of 1939 should be mentioned. The pact provided Stalin with a rationale for his later act of self-delusion. With it he had a formal basis for believing that his country was immune to attack, despite Hitler's record in breaking treaties and agreements. Unquestionably, Stalin's earlier poor judgement buttressed his later self-deception.

In very recent times, the David Irving trial has demonstrated the enormous capacity for self-delusion in the Holocaust denial movement. Irving, a self-styled academic historian of the Third Reich, sued Deborah Lipstadt and Penguin for libel after she accused him, in her book *Denying the*

Holocaust, of being a Holocaust denier. During the trial, a systematic examination of Irving's methodology was conducted. The defence looked carefully at the use that Irving had made of Nazi documents in the many books he had written. This enabled the court to judge whether the defence was right in contending that Irving was a falsifier and distorter of history.

In summing up at the end of the lengthy trial, the judge concluded that Irving had 'treated the historical record in a manner which fell far short of the standard to be expected of a conscientious historian'. He had 'misrepresented and distorted the evidence which was available to him.' But this was not the mere intellectual error into which many historians fall. Irving's distortions were based on strongly held ideological beliefs and racial prejudices. The author's clear anti-Semitism and his powerful pro-Nazi bias had ensured that his mistaken reading of the documents was not accidental. During the trial, Irving had cast doubt on the authenticity of certain documents merely because they 'did not fit in with his thesis'. He had a 'determination to adhere to his preferred version of history, even if the evidence does not support it'. The author's political agenda had disposed him, where necessary, 'to manipulate the historical record in order to make it conform with his political beliefs'.[1] Irving did not just falsify the historical record: he was a wilful denier whose distorted methodology was designed to promote his racist views.[2]

These cases give us a glimpse into the distorted thinking characteristic of self-deception. We should be in no doubt that it can radically distort our world view and have truly pernicious consequences. A number of important questions remain. We need to understand why people deceive themselves, how people deceive themselves and whether the very idea of self-deception is conceptually possible. In the rest of this book, I hope to answer these questions.

'I have done that,' says my memory. 'Impossible,' says my pride and remains inexorable. Finally memory yields.

Nietzsche

Chapter 1

Introducing Self-deception

'When my love swears that she is made of truth,
I do believe her though I know she lies.'

Shakespeare, Sonnet 138

The self-deceiver hides from himself what he believes or strongly suspects to be true because it is too painful for him to avow. In deceiving ourselves, we are both victims and victors. Undoubtedly, self-deception can relieve us of the burden of painful and unpleasant thoughts, helping us to attain a desirable self-image in the face of opposing evidence. But while it may stop us confronting painful parts of our lives, it also prevents us being rational and sincere truth seekers. As one author has recently put it, self-deception involves an 'irony that we may be our own greatest obstacles in a search for self-understanding'.[3] When we are self-deceived, we can no longer pretend to have an accurate perspective on our mental lives. It is therefore a fundamental misrepresentation of ourselves, both to ourselves and to others.

Borrowing the language of Herbert Fingarette, we self-deceive when there is a motivated failure to acknowledge or avow something we have done or something we believe. Self-deception arises from a clash between evidence about

1

our own behaviour, or that of someone to whom we are close, and the implicit commitments, projects and values that we live by. The end result is a form of cognitive dissonance, and ultimately something must give. Some additions to self-knowledge are likely to become elusive when they involve things we would rather not contemplate. Contrary to the counsel of Socrates, not all self-knowledge is equally desirable and, sometimes, the truth does not set you free.

As self-deceivers, we need to shield ourselves from painful and threatening ideas and preserve our self-esteem in more positive ways. It is natural that we should want to de-emphasise our flaws, and believe that we make more than mediocre contributions to the world around us. As David Nyberg puts it, 'We cannot just live; we must live worthily if we can, and *seem* to do so if we can't always.'[4] Eugene O'Neill captured the spirit of this type of self-deception in *The Iceman Cometh*. For one character, Larry, 'the lie of a pipe dream is what gives life to the whole misbegotten mad lot of us, drunk or sober.' The playwright was arguing that sometimes illusions are fundamental to our self-esteem and cannot be removed with impunity. We all seem to shield ourselves from what Ibsen called 'vital lies', and then walk a psychological tightrope between denial and truth. Self-deception is often about *self-protection*, which relies on the preservation of our self-esteem. Self-esteem can be regarded as a survival instinct that needs to be guarded when danger threatens. If we lose it, we also lose the freedom and happiness that illusory hope can provide. Illusion is truly 'compassion's remedy for the disappointment of reality'.[5]

This viewpoint has been supported from within the world of cognitive science. In his article, 'The totalitarian ego: fabrication and revision of personal history', Anthony Greenwald views the self as an information system that can distort information in order to maintain its coherent

2

view of the world. It fabricates and revises one's personal history, and is dominated by cognitive skews which are similar to 'thought control and propaganda devices'. He cites experimental results that seem to show how 'an egocentric bias' pervades mental life. One manifestation of this bias is the way facts are better remembered the more they concern oneself.

Some research has shown that as people gaze at their environment, they are more likely to process and encode self-relevant information. Also prevalent is what Greenwald calls 'the beneffectance bias',* a necessary process of cognitive organisation and self-satisfaction whereby the self deems itself responsible for desired but not undesired outcomes. These biases are pervasive because they are highly adaptive; they help to protect the integrity of the ego. They are also based around a central organising need, namely to encode information in a way that protects the interests of the self.

While self-deception is an all too readily identifiable psychological foible, it remains problematic for philosophical psychology. Taken in its literal form, many philosophers have claimed that self-deception cannot exist at all, arguing that it produces too many counter-intuitive and paradoxical consequences. My aim in this book will be to describe the nature and proximate aetiology of self-deception in a philosophically coherent manner. I will propose a new model for understanding self-deception, one that is not paradoxical, and which shows it to be a purposeful and motivated exercise in irrationality.

The phenomenon of self-deception: How have philosophers conceived of self-deceptive behaviour? I will give three

---

* Anthony G. Greenwald, *The Totalitarian Ego: Fabrication and Revision of Personal History*, American Psychologist 35 (1980): 603–618.

examples of typical self-deceptive behaviour that appear in the recent philosophical literature:

Donald Davidson, firstly, gives the example of Carlos, who has an impending driving test. He has good reasons to believe that he will fail his test. His instructor has made numerous remarks suggesting imminent failure, and recent tests have not been encouraging. The totality of his evidence points to a great likelihood of failure. This thought is painful to him, however, and he therefore has a clear motive (avoidance of pain) to believe the opposite, namely that he will pass the test. He employs a variety of techniques, such as pushing the negative evidence into the background in order to do this. Carlos remains aware that his evidence favours the belief that he will fail, something that continually motivates him to deny this evidence and promote a more favourable belief.

The second example of self-deceptive behaviour comes from an article on self-deception by Frederick Schmitt. I will refer to it as the 'case of the glutton':

'To deceive myself into thinking I'm not a glutton, I might begin with an appreciation of the evidence of my gluttony and propelled by a growing distaste for gluttony, I might arrange my thoughts and observations of my environment in such a way that I come to weigh the evidence and to gather further evidence so as to favour my not being a glutton. I might systematically relax my attention when I recount the episodes in which I overconsume food and I might make a special effort to recall those instances in which I have shown restraint in the consumption of food or abstained from eating when I very much wanted to eat. As a result of the habits I develop in thinking this way, I come to weigh the evidence I possess in favour of my not being a glutton.'[6]

If anyone is truly self-deceived, it is the deluded lover in David Pears' book *Motivated Irrationality*. A girl has

4

sufficient available evidence that her lover is unfaithful, but she refuses to believe this. Her conscious acknowledgement that her partner is a philanderer would be too painful to bear. In her actions, though, it is quite obvious that this belief is acknowledged. She avoids being in certain places where she is certain he is with his lover, and leaves the house when she thinks he will be there with her. She avoids walking to work past a cafe which she strongly suspects is frequented by the pair.

When questioned about these evasive activities, she rationalises her actions and denies any belief about his lack of fidelity. She expresses amazement that anyone could possibly think he was unfaithful, and is disgusted at the thought of him being a philanderer. Given her level of distaste, any rational onlooker would scarcely think that she was feigning ignorance of his activities. Despite her avowed belief in his innocence, it seems obvious that deep down she acknowledges that he is a cheat.

These are typical of the cases of self-deception we encounter in everyday life. Other examples could include: the mother who believes in her son's innocence despite the evidence stacked up against him; the teacher who believes in his exceptional abilities despite his consistently failing students; the cancer patient who disbelieves in the seriousness of his illness; the gambler who denies any harmful addiction to visiting casinos. No doubt, we could multiply such instances from our everyday experience, but the consistent pattern of behaviour seems unmistakable.

Characteristics: These paradigm cases of self-deception have a certain psychological and behavioural pattern in common. They involve, firstly, the motivated possession of a belief that is unsupported by the subject's available evidence. This is what I call the 'favoured' or 'promoted' belief. The glutton desires a positive self-image that centres around her modest lifestyle. She therefore promotes a belief that she has modest eating habits and that she is not a glutton. The deluded lady wants to believe that her partner is faithful and promotes the belief that he is not a philanderer. Carlos believes sincerely that he will pass his impending driving test. All of these promoted beliefs are unsupported by the subjects' available evidence.

The subjects also believe, at some level, the opposite of the favoured belief. This 'unfavoured' but rational belief is one they find deeply unpleasant, though it accords strongly with the agent's available evidence. Its unpleasantness can be traced to the fact that it clashes with a fundamental and strongly held 'goal' to which the person adheres. The glutton's fundamental desire for an image of modest eating habits is violated by her rational belief. The lady's desire for a stable love life would take a huge setback if she accepted the rational belief she possesses. So, too, Carlos' confidence would plummet if he fully accepted a belief that he was likely to fail his driving test. There is a failure of avowal or acknowledgement, but this is motivated, not accidental.

Typically, these agents will act at certain moments as if they genuinely accepted the unfavoured and rational belief. Thus the lady avoids the cafe because she thinks her lover will be there. The glutton may throw away her cookbooks, suspecting strongly that what she finds there will make highly unpleasant reading. Carlos will visibly mull over a negative remark made by his instructor for the same reason. However, it is crucial that as soon as the rational belief enters awareness, the subject erects a suitable defence against it or, as we shall see, there may be subintentional mechanisms that can do this job effectively. Finally, the cases involve the stringent denial of this unfavoured belief, in thought, speech and behaviour.

To sum up these characteristics, self-deception appears to be a purposeful, motivated and irrational exercise in self-misrepresentation, carried out in order to avoid anxiety and maintain self-esteem.

How self-deception seems paradoxical: Despite this, many philosophers believe that self-deception is an inherently nonsensical term. Instead, some argue that the behaviour which does exist needs to be redescribed using words that avoid the sniff of paradox. It is to these paradoxes that we must turn.

The paradoxes of self-deception arise most noticeably when we attempt to model it on interpersonal deception, the deception of one person by another. In other words, the paradoxes follow if we construe self-deception literally, namely as a person's deception of him or herself. The two central paradoxes associated with this literal reading of self-deception are the 'paradox of belief' and the 'strategy paradox'. I will call the attempt to model self-deception on the deception of one person by another the 'two-person model' of self-deception. This is simply because deception involves two or more parties. In order to fully understand the problems with applying this model, let us look in depth at the intricacies of ordinary interpersonal deception.

Interpersonal deception: Like self-deception, deception is integral to human life but is an equally elusive and intriguing concept. There have been a variety of attempts at providing a set of necessary and sufficient conditions for being deceived and for deceiving others, the issue spawning a huge philosophical literature.

The Oxford English Dictionary defines the word 'deception' in the following two ways:

i) To ensnare: to take unawares by craft or guile; to overcome, overreach, or get the better of by trickery: to beguile or betray into mischief or sin; to mislead.

ii) To cause to believe what is false; to mislead as to a matter of fact, lead into error.

The second usage is one we associate less with stereotypical cases of interpersonal deception but is also recognisable in everyday conversation. We talk of being deceived by the light or by the appearance of an object. The object in question that is causing us to be deceived can be non-sentient and, hence, can lack a relevant intention to mislead us. Essentially, the implication of this usage is that we are caused to believe something, albeit temporarily, that is a non-deliberate misrepresentation of reality.

For example, one day I make my weekly visit to the theatre. One of the actors happens to be standing on a part of the stage which is slightly raised. This leads me to think that he is far taller than the other actors. In fact, the actors are all the same height, something I discover when I visit them backstage afterwards. Once this error is revealed, I may claim that the theatrical set-up is deceiving me, in that my perception of the actor was distorted by the stage. My temporary belief that the actor was very tall did not correspond with reality. But the fact that the producer did not intend to dupe me does not stop me saying that 'appearances were deceptive'.

We might wish to extend the notion of 'causing to believe what is false' to human activities. There are innumerable examples of humans being led astray by false reasoning or through a belief system which is untrue but seems rational at the time. Ptolemy held the pre-Copernican belief that the sun revolved around the Earth. In publicly expounding this hypothesis, he was causing other people to have false beliefs. While his audience were deceived with respect to the truth of a proposition regarding the nature of Sun-Earth orbital relations, Ptolemy did not deceive them in the ordinary sense of the term. He had no intention to mislead them or misrepresent reality to them. He simply knew no better.

It is clear that we cannot use the first notion of 'deception by appearances' or the notion of unintentionally causing others to have false beliefs as a basis for understanding self-deception. We likened deception by an object to being caused accidentally to see a non-truthful representation of an object. The reflexive extension of this form of deception would be that we cause ourselves to have non-truthful representations of the environment. But this need not involve self-deception as we understood its characteristics earlier.

Suppose I go to a local newspaper library to check its massive archive. My assignment is to find out the exact starting date of the Falklands War. Owing to poor eyesight, I need glasses but I have forgotten to bring these along with me. I start reading the date on the first newspaper I pick up, recording it as 29th March. Due to defective vision, what I see as a 2 is actually a 1, and the date I should record is the 19th. Here I cause myself to have a false belief, but this is a mere perceptual error, not a case of self-deception. I do not know about my 'self-caused misrepresentation', and thus I am deceived with respect to the Falklands War. The pattern of events just described does not fit with the psychological characteristics mentioned earlier for being self-deceived. As soon as my error is pointed out, there will be no reason for me to persist in my false belief.

Clearly to understand deception in the generally accepted sense of the term, we need to add the notion of intention. The first definition involves, among other things, to 'overcome' or 'overreach', to 'beguile or betray into mischief,' or simply to 'mislead'. This automatically implies the presence of a plan or strategy to mislead another person with respect to some matter of fact. Contrary to a commonly held view, deception or the intention to mislead does not hinge primarily on the truth or falsity of what you say, but on your state of mind. The distinction between truthfulness and deception turns on the intentions of the deceiver, not on the success of what is intended.[7]

It is, in other words, perfectly possible to deceive another party intentionally by making them believe something that happens to be true. Thinking it is now 5.00, I want you to believe it is 5.30 to make you hurry up for an appointment. I tell you that it is 5.30 before you leave the house in a hurry. However, unknown to me, my watch stopped half an hour ago and it is indeed 5.30 at the moment. Naturally, I have not deceived you with respect to the truth of a proposition regarding the time. However, I have straightforwardly deceived you, even though I have told you the truth.

The difference between the two is the deceiver's state of mind. If I genuinely take the world to be a particular way but want you to believe differently, I can be said to have intentionally deceived you. I have not given you a false representation of the world but a false representation of the contents of my mind, namely how I actually take the world to be. We need therefore to spell out the key elements involved in interpersonal deception:

i) x (deceiver) believes p (any proposition), that is, he takes the world to be a particular way.

ii) Another individual (y) is present, an individual that the deceiver recognises as an intentional creature capable of holding beliefs and being persuaded by relevant means to adopt beliefs, not able either to discern the deceiver's intention to deceive or to recognise the 'doxastic disparity'[8] involved in deception.

iii) x has a relevant purpose or reason for deceiving y.

iv) x is aware of and utilises different means of

deceiving. In the case of a lie, this consists of either a verbal or written statement. Deception is a wider term covering different activities.

A set of necessary and sufficient conditions for engaging in interpersonal deception suggest themselves:

i) A believes p on the basis of evidence e, which A believes supports p rather than not p.
ii) A wants B to believe not p rather than p despite evidence e.
iii) A knows that there exists a variety of means by which to produce the belief in B that not p.
iv) A engages intentionally in this deception and gets B to believe not p rather than p, while A believes that p.

Let us examine these closer:

The deceiver has a standpoint on a particular issue, that is, he takes the world to be one way rather than another. It is, therefore, his state of mind rather than the truth or falsity of a proposition held that is used as a reference point in determining whether deception has occurred.

An important component of this condition is that the deception is purposive, with the deceiver having a plan or strategy for engaging in an act of mendacity.

The third condition turns out to be most interesting. There is scope for philosophical debate about the ways that interpersonal deception can be carried out. Clearly, the most straightforward case is that in which, through spoken or written means, I get another to believe a proposition I take to be false – what we call a lie. The classic literary example comes from Shakespeare's *Othello*. Shakespeare brilliantly describes Iago's masterful and crafty acts of mendacity. Iago exaggerates Desdemona's warmth towards

11

Cassio, plays up the extent of her attentions to Cassio, and produces evidence of her infidelity in her motivated plea for Cassio's reinstatement. He knows full well that the basic proposition for which he is seeking Othello's acceptance, 'Desdemona is an adulterer', is false, but is likely to be believed anyway based on the ingenuity of his own subterfuge.

Through his verbal manoeuvring, Iago creates a doxastic disparity between himself and Othello. Iago clearly believes that Desdemona is not an adulterer, while at the same time persuading Othello to believe that she is. At the same time, Iago's intention to create this doxastic disparity (between himself and his deceived victim) is also intentionally hidden. Were this to be given away, Othello would realise that Iago's statements are insincere, thus revealing the deception being practised. In other words, Othello would be colluding in his own deception. Clearly, this is a prime example of saying or writing something despite believing the opposite, the most familiar kind of interpersonal deception.

There are other kinds of ways to achieve the same end. I could deliberately hide evidence that, if it were present, would lead to a certain belief that I do not want another to have. This pattern of deception can be witnessed in Hamlet. Polonius' decision to hide behind the arras when Hamlet enters his mother's bedchamber could be seen as highly deceptive behaviour. He knows that if he does not hide, Hamlet will form the belief that he (Polonius) is present. Polonius does not want Hamlet to have such a belief. By hiding, Polonius reasons that he can create a doxastic disparity between himself (believes that Polonius is present) and Hamlet (believes that Polonius is not present), and that his own intentions will remain hidden.

In this example, we can discern the difference between intentional deception and lying, a difference which centres on the methods used to deceive, not the results gained. A typical lie comes in spoken or written forms and explicitly conveys a message that the deceiver takes to be false. The approach is a more direct one than the subtle misinformation of Polonius, who does not say or write anything, although the effect is equivalent.

Some philosophers believe there are other methods by which to deceive that do not involve proaction. David Nyberg believes that deception, understood as a purposive activity, can be accomplished using at least eight methods:

i) Contribute to causing S to acquire a false belief.
ii) Contribute to causing S to continue in a false belief.
iii) Contribute to causing S to stop believing something true.
iv) Contribute to causing S to be unable to believe something true.
v) Choose to allow S to acquire a false belief.
vi) Choose to allow S to continue in a false belief.
vii) Choose to allow S to stop believing something true.
viii) Choose to allow S to go on without a true belief.

Nyberg says that all these cases involve 'self-awareness, intention, deliberateness and responsibility'.* There seems to be no problem fitting the first four conditions into our account of interpersonal deception. It is the latter four cases, examples of what the author calls 'letting it happen', that are problematic. They seem to involve mere passivity rather than the proaction which characterises intentional deception. This raises an interesting question which Nyberg

---

*David Nyberg, *The Varnished Truth* (Chicago, The Universiy of Chicago Press), p. 95.

is also sensitive to: to what extent are we responsible for another person's belief acquisition when we are in only a remote and indirect position to influence that acquisition?

I know a huge number of tourists will visit London this year. I am also quite sure that many will congregate around Nelson's Column. Furthermore, I happen to know that several times a week, a group of charlatan psychics converge on the area to give a number of bogus 'readings' to the credulous tourists. The latter will end up both deceived and out of pocket. Knowing about the potential deception, I could easily turn up and warn the tourists not to part with their cash. However, I decide to stay at home that day. In some sense, I (among others) let the deception go ahead. In choosing to allow others to be duped, it is arguable that I could be subject to a limited form of moral censure. But my own causal distance from these events seems sufficient for me not to be labelled a deceiver. I am too far removed in the chain of events leading to the actual deception to be a proper part of it. Yet my role is consistent with Nyberg's conditions v) and vi).

To summarise, then, if Jones engages in the intentional deception of Smith, this should be characterised as a deliberate attempt by Jones to mislead Smith with respect to what Jones takes to be the truth of a proposition, thus creating doxastic disparity between Jones and Smith, usually accomplished through spoken or written means (the lie), in which Jones' intentions to deceive remain out of view.

The two-person model: Understood literally, self-deception involves applying what happens in interpersonal deception to what happens in a single person. The person is both deceiver and deceived. As deceiver, he must get himself, as deceived, to believe a proposition that he also believes is untrue. He believes a proposition and, at the same time, he disbelieves it.

14

This idea can be represented schematically:

i) A believes p, usually, but not always, on the basis of evidence e, which A believes to support p rather than not p.

ii) A wants (A) to believe not p rather than p despite evidence e.

iii) A knows if the evidence for p is manipulated or if the evidence for not p is produced, (A) will believe not p rather than p.

iv) A manipulates evidence relevant to the truth value of the belief that p.

v) A therefore gets (A) to believe not p rather than p while also believing p.

Paradoxes of self-deception: There are two central paradoxes thrown up by the two-person model, which are the 'paradox of belief,' and the 'strategy paradox.'

Paradox of belief: From condition v) on the schema, we can see clearly that a self-deceived subject appears simultaneously both to believe and not believe the same proposition. If the person accepts the import of the evidence in condition i), then he believes it supports proposition p rather than not p, and that very acceptance ought to negate his believing not p. If evidence points unambiguously in the direction of a stated belief, it cannot support belief in 'p' as well as its contrary 'not p'. The combination of attitudes presented in the schema appears to be an impossibility. In a case of self-deception, we appear to sin against an important normative principle called 'the requirement of total evidence for inductive reasoning'. This principle, 'enjoins us in a situation of conflict to hold the belief that is best supported'.[9]

We need to be sure just what the paradox of belief

entails. Take the following three statements:

i) At time t, the lady believes that her lover is faithful and she believes that her lover is unfaithful.

ii) At time t, the lady believes that her lover is faithful and unfaithful.

iii) At time t, the lady believes that her lover is faithful and she does not believe that her lover is faithful.

Which of these statements is logically equivalent to the paradox? It does not apply to the second attribution. This alleges that the lady believes one straightforward contradiction, and nothing in her behaviour or verbal utterances at any one moment could motivate this ascription. In the third case, we, the ascribers, are in a contradiction. The paradox lies in the first statement. This ascribes two separate beliefs to the lady which have contradictory contents and logical entailments. When it comes to spelling out the contents and entailments of both beliefs, the lady will eventually contradict herself, assuming that she, as a rational agent, understands the import of the terms in each of the sentences.

Now, we should be clear that the paradox of belief is more than the simultaneous holding of contradictory beliefs. I can believe that 'single men are hirsute' but also believe that 'no bachelor is hirsute'. If I do not realise that bachelors are single men, then my beliefs are in one sense contradictory though I can easily hold them simultaneously. The irrationality of the paradox of belief is that one holds contradictory beliefs subject to a form of motivational bias. One 'avowed' or favoured belief is held in the teeth of contradictory evidence; moreover, it is directly sustained by a partial awareness of the belief that contradicts it. Clearly, if I believe that single men are hirsute, this is not being 'maintained' through my believing anything about bachelors. I have no motive which impels me to believe that single men are hirsute based on my believing that no bachelor is hirsute. If I found out a little more about the meaning of the word 'bachelor', I would alter my statements about the bodily characteristics of single men.

Strategy paradox: A more important problem arises when we consider the actual dynamics of self-deception, the puzzle which we can term the 'strategy paradox.' There is a problem with an agent employing a self-deceptive strategy with the intention of deceiving himself. How can a self-deceiver lie to himself when he knows that this is what he is doing? The project would be utterly self-defeating. The attempted lie to oneself founders on the fact that those things one wishes to conceal from oneself (the belief to be concealed and the evidence it is based on) are not after all concealed. We can see in condition v (page 15) that the subject will still retain the belief that he wishes to disavow, and knowledge of this residual belief will make the project self-defeating. The strategy paradox involves a situation in which a person intends to disavow an undesired belief in order for it not to figure in his consciousness, although he is guided by his awareness of the belief in doing so. Just how can one use one's knowledge in the act of concealment without the knowledge subverting the attempt to conceal? I need to identify that belief or fact about myself prior to my attempting to deny it; what I wish not to see must be seen first of all. Drawing on the analogy with interpersonal deception, we can also say that A cannot deceive B if B knows what A is up to. B would know all that A knows and so would be colluding in the lie A was attempting to perpetrate. Under such circumstances, lying would become impossible.

17

Trying to deceive oneself in this sense appears as problematic as trying to forget something. The more one focuses on the thing to forget, the more the memories recur and the harder the whole enterprise becomes.

The paradox of belief and the strategy paradox suggest that no single subject can simultaneously hold contrary beliefs subject to the motivational bias mentioned. As a result, self-deception, literally construed, appears to be a candidate for elimination from our vocabulary; quite simply, it could not be describing anything in the real world. We shall later see the attempts some philosophers have made to redescribe the phenomena that we commonly think of as self-deception. However, I intend to argue that we can overcome the challenge presented by both of these paradoxes. I will show that self-deception, as literally construed, is less paradoxical than we think, despite surface appearances. Furthermore, it is largely isomorphic with ordinary deception. I will show that my non-paradoxical theory can easily take on board the condition of holding contrary beliefs as well as the strategic element characteristic of much self-deception.

The argument: The structure of my argument will now be outlined. We said earlier that the paradoxes of self-deception arise from the application of the two-person model. Accordingly, there are a number of ways one can treat this model. One could either reject it completely, accept it literally as implying that self-deception must involve one person deceiving another within oneself, or accept its central features without taking them to imply a 'two-person' approach. In chapter 2, I explore a number of attempts by authors to follow the first approach and reject the application of the model. They attempt to show how self-deception in reality assimilates to 'wishful thinking', interpersonal deception, deception over time and related

18

concepts. I will criticise these views for failing to capture the range of characteristics that I believe are central to self-deception.

If we embrace the two-person model literally, we can take one of two options: we can either reject the notion of self-deception as incoherent and illogical, or accept that a radical revision of our ordinary modes of psychological explanation is called for. The latter option may involve the postulation of a homuncular model in which the person can be divided up into a deceiving protective subsystem and a deceived main subsystem. In other words, a literal approach to the model would imply that there are two agents inside the one human head, one a deceiver and another deceived.

Chapter 3 analyses an ingenious attempt made recently by David Pears to resolve the two paradoxes along this line. He suggests that in a case of self-deception, there are two rational centres of agency in the one person's head, a main system which is akin to the person's conscious self, and a protective subsystem. The latter is responsible for perpetrating the deception of the former. I refer to this viewpoint as 'strongly divisive' and as involving 'strong partitioning'. That is, the divisions it introduces into the person's psychic life are radical, as they involve postulating subagents or proto-persons within the subject. This notion of strong partitioning leaves us with several highly counter-intuitive consequences, all of which will be spelled out at the end of the chapter.

I choose a third approach to the two-person model. I believe that the two-person model is a useful model for understanding self-deception. Part of the reason why we have adopted the label 'self-deception' is that some analogies and similarities can be found between cases of interpersonal deception and those of self-deception. The acceptance of these features of the two-person model,

19

however, does not involve thinking of two agents or agent-like entities, one of which deceives the other. At the end of chapter 3, the third approach to the two-person model is spelt out and used to create a better understanding of how self-deception can occur.

In chapter 4, I will outline what I call 'weak self-deception', a category of self-deception in which it is possible to become self-deceived through unintentional self-misrepresentation. In chapter 5, I will discuss how self-deception can occur with the intention of the agent. The intentional techniques of self-deception are then discussed in depth in the remainder of the chapter.

In chapter 6, the solution to the two paradoxes will be spelt out. My theory is one of 'weak partition' as opposed to the strong partitive theory of Pears. The solution to both paradoxes involves the concept of mental distance between functionally distinct and segregated sets of beliefs and intentions. The notion of weak partitioning allows agents to have inconsistent beliefs and, in addition, fail to realise their true intentions in acting. I will attempt to solve both paradoxes in a way that does not resort to Pearsian subsystems. Rather, my explanations will include the notion that we are capable of storing causally efficacious beliefs and intentions to which we lack permanent awareness.

In chapter 7, I will apply the results obtained from the preceding discussion to the presentation of irrationality in Freudian theory. I cite some familiar Freudian case studies, such as the Rat Man and the Tablecloth Lady, and examine whether Freud's characterisation of irrationality can be understood in the familiar terms of self-deception. I will argue that Freudian theory is not committed to the radical compartmentalisation of agency that we find in Pearsian theory. The division of self, for Freud, is not based on the notion of multiple agency. While classic psychoanalytic theory appears to offer a theory of self-deception, it does not work through the same kinds of psychological explanation as we find in common-sense psychology.

Finally, chapter 8 deals with questions about the irrationality of self-deception. I will examine carefully whether self-deceivers are irrational and, if so, in what way. More than one conception of irrationality will be discussed.

Conditions for becoming and being self-deceived: I will now offer a set of conditions or criteria for becoming self-deceived.[10] We can think of a criterion for something's being x as a feature that we must look out for if we can judge that something to be x. Typically, something counts as a criterion for another thing if it constitutes necessarily good evidence for it. While, in many cases, a criterion is a necessary condition for the presence of a property, it need not be absolutely necessary. Thus, the analysis of important philosophical concepts, such as knowledge or truth, may involve the establishment of a set of truth conditions that cover only paradigmatic cases. In the eighteenth century, one of the criteria that was necessary to define a man was that he had a heart, and this functioned effectively at the time. In the twentieth century, however, medical advances have led to men having pacemakers and artificial hearts. The 'heart' criterion therefore is defeasible, remaining open to empirical revision and objection. Criteria, therefore, need not cover every conceivable kind of property or case in question. The criteria that I have put forward are designed to cover the generally accepted cases of self-deception that appear in literature, history and everyday observation. I have set out six conditions for entering self-deception, which are taken to be 'jointly sufficient and severally necessary'.

21

i) Jones encounters and accepts the import of evidence supporting proposition not p rather than p.

ii) As a result, Jones believes not p rather than p.

iii) Jones' believes that not p is unwelcome and he desires that p rather than not p be the case. We can call this the 'core desire'.

iv) Jones' desire for p causes tropistically (unintentionally) the desire to believe that p rather than not p. The desire to believe p rather than not p is called the biasing desire.

v) The biasing desire causes a displacement of the belief that not p in favour of the belief that p. This can happen in one of two main ways: a) It triggers one of a number of self-serving unconscious and unintentional belief-biasing procedures. b) It triggers one of a number of intentional strategies of belief manipulation.

vi) The retention of the new belief, in the face of strong evidence contrary to it, suggests the presence of the rational but unwelcome belief. This belief is still held at some level by the subject, but he does not fully spell it out or avow it. It can be detected later in behaviour.

Throughout this work, I shall refer to the 'propositional attitudes'. The propositional attitudes are, in essence, those mentalistic states whose contents are, in some way, about the world. Propositional attitudes include, but are not confined to, states of belief, desire, hope, fear and intention. To take an example, 'John believes that the cat is on the mat' is a sentence that contains the propositional-attitude state 'belief'. We can say that the belief is about the cat being on the mat, and the content of this attitude can then be expressed in a proposition as above. The influence of propositional-attitude psychology will become apparent throughout.

Chapter 2

Rejecting the Two-person Model

'Self-love is so natural to us that, most often, we never feel it.'

Bernard le Bovier de Fontenelle

In this chapter, I will consider some recent attempts by philosophers to explain self-deception in terms that reject the two-person model. That is to say, they do not understand self-deception as being isomorphic with intentional interpersonal deception. Instead, what we commonly take to be self-deception is assimilated to more familiar and non-paradoxical notions, such as wishful thinking, ordinary deception and deception over time. By choosing to understand the phenomena of self-deception in these terms, the paradoxes appear to have been dispelled. However, I will argue that conceptual clarity is achieved at the expense of losing sight of the very phenomena at issue.

Deception over time: One way to conceive of self-deception without hint of paradox is to regard it as an explicit strategy to deceive oneself that is undertaken over a stretch of time. Alfred Mele illustrates this notion of 'deception over time' with his example of Ike, the prankster:

Ike, a forgetful prankster skilled at imitating others' handwriting, has intentionally deceived friends by secretly making false entries in their diaries. Ike has just decided to deceive himself by making a false entry in his own diary. Cognizant of his forgetfulness, he writes under today's date, 'I was particularly brilliant in class today,' and counts on eventually forgetting that what he wrote is false. Weeks later ... Ike reads this sentence and acquires the belief that he was brilliant in class on the specified day... He intended to bring it about that he would believe that p, which he knew at the time to be false: and he executed that intention without a hitch, causing himself to believe, eventually, that p.[11]

Another famous account of deception over time comes in Pascal's famous 'wager argument'. In order to stave off the evils of atheism, Pascal urged non-believers to act in ways that suggested they believed in God. He urged people to take holy water, go to mass and attend church in the same manner as ordinary believers. He thought that after a certain period of time, people would come to accept that they believed in God simply because this is what their behaviour was suggesting to them, irrespective of what they initially believed.

These cases involve something like the following idea: one holds a belief p at time t that one takes to be supported by one's available evidence. However, for a given reason, one wishes to believe the contrary, the belief that not p. One decides that the best course of action to adopt is to strategically induce in oneself the belief that not p so that it will be believed at some time in the future – time t1. This scheme will only work if one is able to forget that the belief that not p one has at time t1 was the result of planned manipulation at time t.

While such methods no doubt have some efficacy in inducing beliefs, the end result is not self-deception. The idea of deception over time leaves no room for the necessary state of psychological tension, motivated inconsistency and contrary beliefs that we find in self-deception. When Ike believes he was brilliant in class on a previous day, he thinks and acts sincerely but has no irrational motivation for this belief. But if Ike were self-deceived, he would be motivated to believe he was brilliant only by suppressing the belief that he was in reality a poor student. It is only through the occasional awareness of being poor that a self-deceived Ike would be motivated to believe such a positive self-assessment. Ike's state of knowledge and belief (post forging) would indicate a lack of internal conflict or inconsistency that is always apparent in the self-deceiver. He has only one belief about his performance and abilities, not two.

The argument from avowal/belief discrepancy: In an attempt to escape the paradox of belief, Robert Audi tries to give an account of self-deception that falls short of ascribing contradictory beliefs to a person. In his account, a person S is self-deceived with respect to proposition p if and only if:

1) S unconsciously knows that not p (or has reason to believe that not p);
2) S sincerely avows, or is dispensed to avow sincerely, that p; *and*
3) S has at least one want that explains, in part, both why S's belief that not p is unconscious and why S is disposed to avow that p...[12]

Elsewhere in discussions of case examples, Audi talks of a self-deceiver 'realising' that p when being self-deceived in

25

respect to p. Now, we need to ask whether such descriptions as 'sincerely avow' and 'being dispensed to avow' are as dissimilar to belief as Audi makes out. A sincere avowal after all involves something like an expression of genuine belief.

However, there is surely no implausibility in the idea of grading one's strength of belief. In this sense, sincere avowals of a proposition are manifestations of a weakened form of belief. So a sincere avowal of p can count as a sign of a weaker form of belief that p. At the weaker end of the scale, the subject may strongly suspect rather than sincerely avow that p, but refuse to follow up a suspicion that would, in other circumstances, lead him to the belief that p. There are certainly stronger and weaker cases of doxastic contradiction involved in self-deception. However, typical cases suggest that we could describe self-deception as involving the simultaneous holding of equally held beliefs.

Self-deception as belief in belief-adverse circumstances: Canfield and Gustafson also reject the two-person model for self-deception. They think that, 'All that happens in self-deception ... is that the person believes and forgets something in (belief-adverse) circumstances.'[13] These are circumstances which point the self-deceiver to a belief which very much opposes the one he ought to adopt. The self-deceiver is one who believes something erroneously that it is unreasonable to believe. One of the circumstances that may be adverse to forming correct beliefs is that one is under some form of strong emotional pressure. The above description leaves out the central notions of radical inconsistency, doxastic contradiction and motivated ignorance that are central to the two-person model.

Now it should be clear that there are numerous instances of 'belief in belief-adverse circumstances' that do not involve any kind of self-deception. Jones has just been told that his wife is having an affair. In a fit of jealous rage, he pays a visit to her workplace, convinced that she is having the affair with a work colleague. When he finds her, she is enjoying a friendly chat with a man who, unbeknown to him, is her boss. He immediately forms the belief that she has cheated on him with this man. Jones comes to hold his belief under highly belief-adverse circumstances, namely the influence of his strong jealous rage. Were he not experiencing clear emotional distress, he would be able to interpret the meeting somewhat differently and would not arrive so rapidly at this erroneous conclusion. For Jones, there are belief-adverse circumstances that mar his attempt to acquire evidentially sound beliefs, given his available evidence. Yet we do not have a case of self-deception here. Jones at least is prepared to confront a suspicion, albeit irrationally, rather than place a benign interpretation on some painful facts.

Self-deception as wishful thinking: Self-deception has often been likened to a simple case of wishful thinking. Patrick Gardiner suggests that self-deception amounts to, 'being mistaken with a motive'. According to Gardiner, 'a self-deceiver is simply a man who wrongly believes something to be true which he would not have believed to be true in the absence of the particular interest in the matter concerned...'[14] Gardiner believes that self-deception therefore must be likened to wishful thinking.

We are guilty of wishful thinking when we believe something is the case, in the absence of any evidence, simply because we desire that thing to be the case. George has a strong interest in the hypothesis that humans possess ESP, and wishes to believe that they do indeed possess paranormal powers. However, he has never accumulated or examined any evidence that would support the belief. He believes, nonetheless, that ESP exists. His belief is held purely wishfully, as it has not been subjected to the normal rationally acceptable evidential constraints. In the absence of a desire for ESP to exist, and the consequent absence of a desire to believe in ESP, it is unlikely he would adopt such a belief.

To some extent, this wish-fulfilment model is reflected in the model of self-deception offered in the first chapter. The basic cause of the self-deceptive belief that p is the desire for p that, in turn, causes the desire to believe that p. In wish fulfilment, a person's desire for p does not require any exercise of reason to cause him to desire to believe that p.

The difference between wishful thinking and self-deception, however, is one of kind and not just degree. For self-deception must involve belief which is held *in the teeth of* contrary evidence, evidence which would suggest to any rational person that the opposite belief alone is warranted. This clearly need not be the case with wishful thinking. For all we know, George may possess a correct belief concerning ESP. The point is that his belief is irrational because it has not been adopted via a reliable evidentially based route, i.e. it is not based on proper factual and experimental considerations. A self-deceiver will persist in his belief, finding ways to come to terms with opposing and conflicting evidence. The wishful thinker by definition will not possess opposing evidence.

Failure of introspection: Raphael Demos offers us an intriguing analysis of self-deception. He argues that when we reflect on the apparent inconsistency of accepting a proposition and its negation, we fail to realise that there is a difference between two kinds of awareness: simple awareness and awareness without attending or noticing. The self-deceiver can be aware, in a simple sense, of his belief that p without properly focusing on it or its implications. The failure to do so allows him openly to acknowledge a belief that not p simply because he is not in a position to compare it with another belief that p. Thus there is really no inconsistency in believing that p and not p at the same time.

Despite its initial plausibility, the suggestion that Demos makes is inadequate for explaining self-deception. Firstly, the account excludes mention of the essential motivational feature of self-deception. By describing what happens in self-deception as the outcome of a lack of recognition of beliefs based on a theory of dual levels of consciousness, Demos' characterisation is closer to forgetfulness or error. The individual simply fails to introspect with due care. We infer this much when Demos suggests that the self-deceiver essentially 'fails to notice' or 'is distracted from' a belief. When an individual is in error in this way, we should be successful in pointing out his errors and overruling his judgement. The individual should rationally adjust his beliefs in the light of what we say because he lacks any motive for doing otherwise. This does not happen in self-deception, where the irrational and promoted beliefs are not errors but motivated beliefs held in the teeth of contradictory evidence.

Above all, what is missing from Demos' account is a description of the person's conflicted state. Despite his verbal assurances that he is in a state of psychic harmony, the self-deceived individual is torn between his sincere avowals and his secret and occasional recognition of the painful truth. Demos' characterisation is therefore a failure.

Self-deception as a wavering between hypotheses: Self-deception could be construed as nothing more than a confusing metaphor for the person who wavers between different and contrary hypotheses. Thus, in our initial example, we could say that the lover is caught between thinking that her lover is cheating on her and then thinking that he is the model of fidelity. She is said to be in two minds, uncertain as to which hypothesis she should accept and refusing to commit herself rationally one way or the other.

This suggestion ignores a crucial feature of self-deception, namely the person's sincere conviction that they believe only *one* thing and that any pretence of conflict is superficial. Self-deceivers refuse to conceive of themselves as psychologically conflicted. They have an established belief that they publically refuse to scrutinise, whereas waverers necessarily vacillate over which belief to adopt. Since waverers are those who by definition are unsure, tentative and irresolute in the holding of a given hypothesis, it is inappropriate to think of them as being self-deceived.

Mele's deflationary approach: According to Mele, 'the attempt to understand self-deception as largely isomorphic with paradigmatic interpersonal deception is fundamentally misguided.' His position is 'deflationary': he describes self-deception in a way that is 'neither irresolvably paradoxical nor mysterious and it is explicable without the assistance of mental exotica'.[15] Mele offers these four jointly sufficient conditions for entering self-deception:

1. The belief that p which S acquires is false.
2. S treats data relevant, or at least seemingly relevant, to the truth value of p in a motivationally biased way.
3. This biased treatment is a non-deviant cause of S's acquiring the belief that p.
4. The body of data possessed by S at the time provides greater warrant for not p than for p.[16]

Before presenting an objection to Mele, I will try to relate

30

his account to mine. We will look at some of his conditions in reverse order in order to do so.

The fourth condition states quite clearly that the person's available evidence ought to lead him to a belief that p. Even though Mele does not accept that the person need believe what is consistent with the evidence, he at least agrees that there is 'warrant' for the belief, given the implications of the evidence in question. The second condition is the key one for our accounts, especially the notion of a motivationally biased treatment of data. He states that desiring that p can lead to our believing that p, given a desire-influenced treatment of data. This is already very close to the idea of the core desire and the biasing desire playing an important role in affecting our beliefs. Motivational bias requires the core and biasing desires, and the idea of unintentional mechanisms that can operate at a subdoxastic level to bias our beliefs. These are met in my conditions iii–v (page 22).

Mele renounces the modelling of self-deception on the interpersonal model. He therefore rejects the view that all self-deceivers need to believe something true and then cause themselves to believe its contrary. Utilising the idea of cold or unintentional biasing of beliefs, he argues for four ways in which our desiring that p can lead to our believing that p in instances of self-deception. According to Mele, a desire-influenced treatment of data means that the person will not acquire a given true belief while simultaneously possessing a false one. His four ways are:

i) Negative misinterpretation: S's desiring that p may lead S to misinterpret as not counting against p (or as not counting strongly against p) data which, in the absence of the desire that p, he would easily recognise to count against p.

ii) Positive misinterpretation: S's desire for p may

31

lead S to interpret as supporting p data which count against p, and which, without this desire, S would easily recognise to count against p (if he considered the data).

iii) Selective focusing: S's desiring that p may lead him either to fail to focus his attention on evidence counting against p or to focus instead on evidence suggestive of p.

iv) Selective evidence-gathering: S's desiring that p may lead him both to overlook easily obtained evidence for not p and to find evidence for p which is much less accessible.[17]

According to Mele, 'In none of the examples offered does one hold the true belief that not p and then intentionally bring it about that one believes that p.'[18] As a result, he disagrees that there is any paradoxical state of affairs in which one either holds contrary beliefs simultaneously or has one belief which causes one to adopt the opposite belief while maintaining the first.

Objection to Mele: Mele accepts that the weight of evidence that a person possesses should logically lead him to believe something unfavourable. Yet the agent treats data relevant to the truth value of such a belief in a motivationally biased way. Where does this motivational bias spring from? If the self-deceived agent receives a set of unambiguous data, this should lead inferentially to an unfavoured belief. Why therefore is there a deviation in normal inferences from data to rational belief if not because the data in question are seen to support an unfavoured belief? Clearly, the evidence makes the self-deceiver apprehensive, fearful or anxious, and this is the basis for promoting a favoured belief instead.

Mele believes simply that 'motivation can prime

mechanisms for the cold biasing of data in us, without our being aware, or believing, that our evidence favours a certain proposition.'[19] While this model is not inconceivable, it appears no longer to be a description of self-deception but of wishful thinking. Mele may want to say that the individual has only a marginal awareness of the threatening evidence suggesting an unfavoured belief. If that is the case, however, it does not fit well with self-deception. For as we saw in chapter 2, if the individual does not appreciate the weight of contrary evidence, he cannot really be self-deceived in any sense.

I am prepared to admit that there might be a continuum of cases lying between wishful thinking and self-deception. The characterisation of any one case will depend on the strength of and acceptance of one's evidence for a given belief. The greater a person's evidence for and subsequent acceptance of an unfavoured belief, concurrent with his strong desire for the opposite, the more likely he is to be self-deceived. There would seem to be little reason for the person to persist in his delusional thinking if not for his partial awareness of the rational but unfavoured belief.

Self-deception as interpersonal deception: It has been suggested by some that self-deception is nothing but a clever game carried out by individuals to deceive others. This is what Szabados dubs the 'conspiracy theory' of self-deception. According to the conspiracy theorists, self-deceivers are interpersonal liars who cannot bear the thought of admitting to 'us' the proposition they dread. So they set about lying, denying and being evasive in an effort to divert our attention away from what they really believe. According to this theory, self-deception is nothing more than a confusing metaphor for someone who deceives others.

In many cases, it is certainly true that interpersonal

33

relations are important to the maintenance of self-deception. Fundamental to the whole irrational project is the need to maintain strong self-esteem and to preserve the integrity of the ego. Clearly the pleasant and morale-boosting appraisals of some of our peers can help us to achieve this, both in rational and irrational contexts. If our friends and colleagues help us to develop a pleasant belief about ourselves, they can arguably help to keep us self-deceived. It is easier to believe something if it is confirmed strongly and persuasively by people whose opinions we value.

While the conspiracy theory appears to have much to commend it, it exaggerates the role of other people. It is true that our deceiving ourselves may lead to the deception of others and multiply the number of misled agents. More often than not, however, it is our friends and colleagues who see through our disguises, candidly advising us to look at a situation with their lucidity and neutral detachment. Friends can point out unwelcome facts, see through our clever half-truths, and urge us to confront the fearful situation that seemingly we cannot face. Thus we should not be surprised if the deluded lover is told by her friends that her lover is not the model of fidelity that she would like to believe. The glutton is perceived by her peers to be in the grip of a delusion about her weight. Friends of alcoholics confront, rather than accept, the psychological denials they observe.

If we are playing a subtle game with our peers, attempting to perpetrate a clever fraud to save face in their presence, then we are all too often unsuccessful. Our attempts at deceiving others, as in ordinary lying, cannot succeed unless we can see that others are being actively duped by us. If we create lies and our victims find out about our deception, our strategy falls flat. Despite the remonstrations of their peers, self-deceivers remain in the grip of their irrationality.

In conclusion, the attempt to model self-deception by rejecting the two-person model and assimilating it instead to such notions as deception over time, wavering between contrary hypotheses, interpersonal deception or wishful thinking, is doomed to failure. We can now examine an alternative approach to understanding self-deception, one based on the straightforward equation of self-deception with interpersonal deception via the literal acceptance of the two-person model.

Chapter 3

Pears and Partition

'The heart has reasons that reason does not understand.'

Jacques Beninge Bossuet

A radically different approach to irrationality is provided by David Pears. Pears takes the second approach to the two-person model, explaining self-deception literally in terms of one agent deceiving another agent. We will see that this approach is also flawed and highly counter-intuitive.

Pears is one of the leading exponents of a strongly partitive explanation of irrationality. We should be clear exactly what we mean by a 'partitive explanation'. In a case of self-deception, it is thought intuitively that the person divides into a deceiving and a deceived part, each in possession of a set of propositional attitudes.[20] There would therefore exist, as Sebastian Gardner says, 'relations of inconsistency between propositional attitudes'.[21] The alcoholic who is aware of his condition and who is self-deceived in believing that he is not an alcoholic will consciously believe that he is not an alcoholic. However, it is thought that another part of him possesses a different set of propositional attitudes, among which is the belief that he is an alcoholic. When he later comes to examine the

36

cause of his irrationality, he may point out that it had to be found in a motive force within himself. In other words, there was a mental part that was responsible for deceiving him.

So we should understand a partitive explanation of irrationality to be one that accounts for irrationality by dividing the person into mental parts. We need to distinguish between 'weak' and 'strong' forms of partitioning which correspond to strong and weak conceptualisations of these mental parts. The notion of 'weak partitioning' of the self can be understood in terms of an innocent split within the one agent between his accessible and inaccessible mental states. This theory of the irrational mind is based on the idea that a subject's beliefs or intentions can become temporarily segregated, falling into distinct regions of the mind. This notion will be examined in greater depth in chapter 6.

Pears' account divides the personal agent in a stronger and more counter-intuitive way. His theory of strong partition conceives of the mind as split into mental parts that strongly resemble persons or rational centres of agency. The difference between strong and weak partition is that, in the former case, we have mental parts as agents or agent-like entities and, in the latter case, we have mental parts constituted by sets or collections of propositional attitudes.

Pears' strongly partitive explanation of self-deception: According to Pears, what happens in a genuine case of self-deception is that the self-deceiver, under the influence of a wish, forms a belief unsupported by his available evidence. According to Pears, only in a scenario where the individual is competent to avoid being irrational need a subsystemic analysis apply. The following three conditions must hold:

i) One mental state causes another in a way that violates a rational constraint.
ii) The subject has the capacity to prevent or correct the causation (competence).
iii) The subject has a belief to the effect that the causation violates a rational constraint.

In the first condition, a wish intervenes in the mind to help form a belief with no rational connection to any of the subject's other propositional attitudes. This is similar to what I called the 'biasing desire'. Pears calls the third belief the 'cautionary belief'. If the lady acknowledged the cautionary belief, then she would believe that her desire for a particular state of affairs to be the case was wishfully biasing her belief system. Naturally, if she was conscious of how her beliefs (taken to be accurate reflections of reality) were influenced and distorted by her desires, in the teeth of counter-evidence, she could no longer deceive herself.

Pears makes a distinction between the permissive and productive causes of irrationality. The permissive cause would identify that mental factor which allows irrationality to occur. The productive cause is that element which fails to prevent irrationality from occurring. Pears believes that we need a theory of the productive cause of self-deception. According to conditions i and ii, the person should be capable of recognising through the cautionary belief that the mental causation is irrational. The mystery for Pears is just why the cautionary belief remains inert and fails to engage the individual sufficiently. This is the point of entry for a strongly partitive subsystemic theory.

Pears postulates a dichotomy between a main system and a protective subsystem within a person. To postulate such a subsystem in the person's mind is to separate a set of propositional attitudes from the majority that are present in the main system. The main system contains a set of desires, beliefs, goals and intentions that are mutually coherent and combine in rational ways to produce further beliefs, desires and actions. In the earlier example the main system contains the lady's accessible beliefs, including both the favoured belief that her lover is faithful and her desire for him not to be unfaithful. It does not contain the cautionary belief, namely that her desire for his faithfulness causes her to adopt an unwarranted belief in his good nature. The cautionary belief would have prevented her believing irrationally that he was not a cheat if only it had integrated with the main system. The protective subsystem's task is to hive away the anxiety provoking cautionary belief and the unfavoured belief and any related propositional attitudes.

Now, the mere postulation of such a schism in the person – in other words a compartmentalisation thesis – is a reiteration of the fact of irrationality. It is 'another piece of theatre',[22] or simply, 'a technical way of restating the facts to be explained'.[23] The thesis at this stage is based around the notion of mental distance. It postulates that certain propositional attitudes, such as the cautionary belief, are withheld from the main system, which explains how irrationality can occur. It is clearly not enough to cite mental distance between these various mental systems; we need to explain how this distance arises. The explanation for the inertness of the cautionary belief is intimately bound up with the identity of the subsystem as a rational agent, or as a rational centre of agency. In other words, the thesis of subsystemic partition needs to be substantiated by examining the nature of the subsystems themselves. Pears writes as follows in *Motivated Irrationality*:

> The subsystem is built around the nucleus of the wish for the irrational belief and it is organised like a person ... it is, from its own point of view, entirely rational.[24]

Pears exploits the analogy of subsystems and persons by considering the former as rational centres of agency. The subsystem is like a rational agent insofar as it is portrayed as having a reason to act and to cause the inertness of the cautionary belief by removing it from the main system. The subsystem not only prevents the main system from being aware of the cautionary belief but also promotes the irrational but favoured belief in the main system. The protective subsystem is conceived as a paternalistic agency, able to protect the main system from an awareness of disturbing thoughts or ideas. The main system, therefore, is affected by the subsystem by virtue of its (subsystem's) identity as a rational agent.

In accordance with its wishful nature, the protective subsystem has a motivated capacity for manipulating the main system. To do this, it must have complete access to the experiences or by-products of experience (e.g. memories) of the main system, so as to decide on its next course of action. In other words for the protective subsystem to be a rational 'belief former', it would have to rationally assess the evidence it finds in the main system. Pears says that we must accept a principle that a system can react to a belief or a desire in another system without necessarily sharing it. According to Pears, it 'would merely take note of its presence ... it would not have to choose between believing and disbelieving it.'[25]

How might the protective subsystem achieve its aim of deceiving the main system? Pears says that the protective subsystem, being a rational centre of agency, has a complex set of beliefs and desires about the main system. It uses these to plot its various strategies in order to produce the favoured and protective belief. It does this either by distracting the main system from believing the anxiety-producing belief, or by rationalising or evading the evidence that supports the belief.

Returning to Pears' case, the girl will avoid a source of evidence that fails to reinforce a cherished image of her love life. The image she desires will consist of a loving, trustworthy and faithful partner. She may imagine that others who are suggesting the opposite are actively conspiring against her. The lady's subsystem will distract the lady's main system from unfavourable evidence about her lover. The subsystem will distract the main system from its normal process of inference and the adoption of any such beliefs as are warranted by the evidence. The subsystem will aim to dominate the main system by implanting a rationalising belief in the main system. As the main system is a gullible victim of the protective system's projects, it would accept the rationalisation thrown at it by the protective subsystem, without realising the source of this rationalisation.

The paradox of belief is solved by saying that the main system possesses one belief and the protective subsystem the other. The strategy paradox is solved by saying that the main system does not plot its own deception; this is due to the deceptive work of the subsystem. Below is a schematic representation for Pears' explanation of self-deception.

i) The lady encounters evidence e that she believes to support p rather than not p.

ii) As a result, the lady believes p rather than not p.

iii) The lady believes that p is unwelcome and has a desire that not p rather than p be the case.

iv) Her desire for not p causes the desire to believe that not p.

v) This desire clashes with the rational belief that p and (owing to its incompatibility with this and other logically related attitudes) causes the lady's mind to divide into a protective subsystem and a main system.

41

vi) The subsystem desires that the main system believe that not p.

vii) The subsystem believes that if it manipulates evidence relevant to the truth value of p, the main system will believe that not p.

viii) The subsystem engages in evidential manipulation, getting the main system to believe not p while overall believing that the evidence supports p.

There are certainly similarities between our theories that should be pointed out. Both Pears and I stress the motivated nature of self-deception. We both rule out 'cold' or unmotivated forms of irrationality, where no motive is centrally cited as the cause of self-deception. The productive cause is akin to the biasing desire in my conditions. For both of us, it is essential that the goal of self-deception is a belief and that the person comes to believe something against the evidence that he possesses. The function of self-deception in our accounts is also similar. Self-deception serves to reduce anxiety or unpleasantness caused by a belief we should rationally adopt, given our available evidence.

Pears' account seems promising. He appears to have removed the air of paradox and then described something that looks exactly like self-deception. In reality, however, he has done this only by bypassing our normal modes of psychological explanation and revising our ideas about how we explain irrationality. We need to see just why his theory is untenable.

THE AETIOLOGY OF THE SUBSYSTEM: Firstly, Pears faces a crucial problem in explaining just how the subsystem is created at all. According to Pears, the motivational force that brings the subsystem to life is a basic wish in the main system. In the case of the lady, it

42

would be the desperate wish that her partner is not a philanderer. The wish not to form the distressing belief about partner infidelity is allowed 'to secede and set up a subsystem in which it becomes the wish that the main system should not form it'.[26] The protective subsystem is created by a powerful wish in the main system, and this wish subsequently motivates the subsystem in all its operations.

The problem starts when one tries to explain how a segregated wish can *become* a subsystem. The wish would essentially need to be invested with agent-like qualities. It would have to envisage the setting up of a special semi-altruistic subsystem as a desirable means of helping the main system. To do this, it would need certain beliefs about the best way to create a subsystem. It would need the necessary prior knowledge, in terms of an envisaged strategy, of enabling its secession to occur from the main system. If this is construed as an intentional act, then it must have a relevant belief about how the secession can take place and perhaps how to evade the probings of the main system. Quite simply, we would need to invest the wish with a high degree of deceptive intent and knowledge.

This is a bizarre notion, for a wish is not itself a rational agent. A wish is simply a mental state which is an intrinsic part of the pattern of rational agency characteristic of a human mind. Even if the self-deceiver is ultimately capable of grasping the potential of a subsystem and setting one up as a result, there seems to be no explanatory advantage gained in subsystemic explanation. For all the relevant work in allowing oneself to be deceived will have been done by the 'agent' who delegates the job of self-deception to a 'part' of himself. The main system, and its beliefs, would be actively aiding one of its own wishes to set up a wishful subsystem, actually colluding in its own deception.

43

Gardner makes the suggestion that 'subsystems are always present in personality, in some actual or immanent form.'[27] This would clear up Pears' difficulties with the causal genesis of the subsystem. We could explain the origin of the special mental distance required of self-deception by postulating that the human personality was structurally divided into opposing goal-driven entities. The acts of internal irrationality that ensue, according to this explanation, would not require the special generation of a subsystem prior to irrational belief formation. Irrationality would be seen to occur against the background of pre-existing goal-bound structures that shape the ways in which we are psychically divided when irrational.

The cost involved in such an explanation is that no proper distinction can be made between explanations of mental disunity and conflict in rational and irrational contexts. The theory of the permanency of subsystems is akin to a cognitive account of self-deception that overlooks the causal role of motive forces within the person. Such motive forces (core and biasing desires) arise at a particular moment in a subject's life and are far from having any psychological permanence.

In the final analysis, Pears' theory violates Ockham's razor. This principle, also known as the principle of parsimony, is a methodological principle of simplicity that states that one should not multiply entities beyond those that are necessary to explain a given phenomenon. The postulation of subagential subsystems therefore requires a radical revision of standard modes of mentalistic explanation and is ultimately gratuitous.

By postulating little agents to run the whole self-deception affair, Pears needlessly multiplies the entities that are relevant to explaining self-deception. The language of subsystems goes beyond what is required, for we could just as easily explain the phenomenon in terms of a clash

44

between different sets of mutually opposed propositional attitudes.

ONE MIND OR TWO: Pears' theory also seems to clash with intuitions we have concerning personal unity and agency. We do not believe that we manifest more than one mind in our one body, even if we know we have been deceiving ourselves. In other words, we do not take our 'self' to be only an individual instance of a multiplicity of selves. We can call this a principle of personal indivisibility. This is an attitude that both shapes our lives and renders our talk of 'being divided' or 'at war with ourselves' merely a useful metaphor for psychologically conflicted states. Pearsian subsystemic theory is at radical odds with this intuition. The subsystems are to be taken as rational centres of agency modelled on individual rational persons. They are envisaged as agencies having thoughts, action dispositions and intentions.

Pears could accept that his subsystemic approach violates notions of personal unity, but he could still demand that we overhaul our intuitions in consideration of self-deception. On this point, empirical research suggesting the compartmentalisation of agency could be cited.

People under hypnosis are often considered to be radically psychologically 'divided'. One part of the person carries out the hypnotist's instruction while the other part is seemingly oblivious to this instruction. In automatic writing, similarly it appears that one part of a person writes something while another part carries out an altogether different task. The enormous evidence for unconscious information processing has also been used to justify the compartmentalisation of agency. We are all aware that solutions to our deep problems can come to us in dream states when they have been inaccessible to introspection.

45

The case of Kekule's dream of the Benzene ring is most famous in this regard. We might be tempted to ascribe the work that has been done in such a case to an unconscious actor who satisfies our cravings below the threshold of consciousness.

In cases of multiple personality, such as the case described in *The Three Faces of Eve* by Drs Thigben and Cleckley, the original subject, Eve White, suffered numerous incidences of psychical disintegration and 'splitting' at moments of great emotional distress. At such times, she would begin to manifest different personalities, each apparently possessing different emotional traits and subject to different action dispositions. As a result of extensive therapy, she was told that her multiplicity came about through a defensive mechanism erected to ward off painful feelings. Insofar as her sense of personal unity in self-consciousness was contravened, she could be said to manifest something akin to multiple selfhood. Such cases, however, do not prove there is anything like a duality of agencies or minds within the one body.

Such an inference is ill-founded as long as we accept that consciousness might fail to reveal how we are unified in very important respects. As Gardner puts it, 'Multiple personality contravenes personal unity only if Cartesian self-consciousness is that in which personal indivisibility consists, or the unique ground of inference to it.'[28] People can, in other words, have incoherent thoughts, feelings or emotions without this contravening their status as basic, indivisible beings. People can simply be unaware of what happens at unfamiliar levels of mental processing.

DECEPTION REVISITED: Another difficulty is that the 'two agent' approach appears to be a blatant account of deception. In Pears' account of self-deception, we seem to remove any basis for describing a state of self-deception.

We have instead a description of the actions or pseudo-actions of two different agents, each equipped with intentions and action plans. Pearsian subsystems have unique, individual thoughts, wishes and action dispositions, and manifest their own standpoints on the world. The strategy of the subsystem will be reflected in the avowals of the main system. However, any verbal thought or representation of the former cannot be ascribed truly to the main system, for the voice that speaks it belongs to another agent, one which manipulates the main system for its own purposes. The main system is a dummy and the subsystem a clever ventriloquist. There is certainly a problem in describing this as self-deception. Self-deception must involve avoidable ignorance or, as Pears would say, a competence to avoid irrationality.

RESPONSIBILITY: The final problem with the Pearsian model is that it absolves the self-deceiver of any responsibility for what he or she does. There are often mitigating circumstances in which self-deceptive projects could be warranted, just as there are circumstances in which it is permissible for us to lie. More often than not, however, the opposite is true. One may try to conceal from oneself knowledge of an act for which one is culpable. It is not unknown for self-deceivers to be accused of mental cowardice, of fleeing from anxiety or danger and lacking the courage to face up to their own problems. Sartre famously accuses self-deceivers of being in 'blind faith' and refusing to face up to the engagements that they have made in the world.

The Pearsian picture, however, portrays self-deceivers as the victims of the cunning activity of the subsystem. If this is the case, then self-deceivers are surely innocent of any charge of wilful ignorance, neglect of rationality or 'bad faith'. Put simply, the Pearsian picture does not allow us to describe self-deception in familiar moral categories. Overall, Pears' account fails to explain the origin of the subsystem and unnecessarily reifies a psychological conflict that should ultimately be explained on the level of a single agent. It also violates strongly held intuitions that we hold concerning our basic personal unity and indivisibility. For the above reasons, Pears' theory represents an inadequate and implausible treatment of self-deception.

Reformulating the two-person model – a third approach: We have seen that the attempts to discredit the two-person model (chapter 2) and to model it using strongly divisive subsystems (chapter 3) leave us with inadequate conceptual accounts of self-deception. In my view, a third position is called for which is able to incorporate most of the key features of the two-person model.

If we assume at the outset that self-deception must be understood purely on a lexical basis, i.e. based rigidly on the dictionary definition of deception, then we run the risk of closing off the debate at the outset. We would be relying on incorporating every standard feature of deception within the self-deception model, so that the one concept was simply based on a reflective extension of the other. Little room would be left for any interpretative debate.

My approach is far more example driven. I have looked at the standard cases of self-deception, attempting to glean their essential behavioural characteristics as a basis for constructing my own explanatory model. The debate over whether to take a lexical or example-based approach to self-deception is a debate over explanation. Self-deception helps to describe and explain a range of behavioural data which we encounter in everyday life. If we find that this data should not be explained by a model that cites little agents dancing inside one's head, self-deception, as Mele puts it, 'would not disappear from our conceptual map'.[29] I believe that there are at least three main parts of the two-person model that can be kept for our description of self-deception:

<u>A wants (A) to believe not p rather than p despite evidence e</u>: This describes the motivated aspect of self-deception. Self-deception serves the goals and desires of the subject, just as deception serves the purposes of the liar.

<u>A manipulates evidence relevant to the truth value of the belief that p</u>: This suggests that the person does something to the evidence which is relevant to the truth value of the proposition one self-deceptively holds. But see below.

<u>A has belief p and brings it about that he believes not p</u>: The self-deceiver misrepresents to himself what he takes to be the case with the world. He also is left with both the initial belief and then the contrary belief.

The one central difference between the two-person model and my reformulated two-person model concerns the notion of intentional action. We saw earlier that interpersonal deception, as we would commonly understand it, had to be fully intentional. Iago did not accidentally or unintentionally deceive Othello with respect to Desdemona. He acted intentionally and was fully aware of his mendacity. The resultant condition iv on page 15 was that the individual manipulated evidence relevant to the truth value of the belief in p. Here, manipulation connotes the kind of strategicality and rational thought that is appropriate to standard cases of interpersonal deception. If we therefore fully apply this model to understand self-deception, we would need to incorporate this feature of intentional action, thus ensuring that there can be no such thing as unintentional self-deception. As I will argue that there are cases where one can deceive oneself through unintentional processes of belief biasing, this condition needs to be dropped from my reformulation of the two-person model.

It is worth reminding ourselves of the terms and conditions for becoming self-deceived as laid out in the Introduction:

i) Jones encounters and accepts the import of evidence supporting proposition not p rather than p.

ii) As a result, Jones believes not p rather than p.

iii) Jones' belief that not p is unwelcome and he has a desire that p rather than not p be the case. We can call this the 'core desire.'

iv) Jones' desire for p causes tropistically (unintentionally) the desire to believe that p rather than not p. The desire to believe p rather than not p is called the biasing desire.

v) The biasing desire causes a displacement of the belief that not p in favour of the belief that p. This can happen in one of two main ways: I) It triggers one of a number of self-serving unconscious and unintentional belief biasing procedures. II) It triggers one of a number of intentional strategies of belief manipulation.

vi) The retention of the new belief in the face of strong evidence contrary to it, suggests the presence of the rational but unwelcome belief. This belief is still held at some level by the subject but he does not fully spell it out or avow it. It can be detected later in behaviour.

It remains to be seen how these conditions can be fitted into the overall theory of self-deception.

Chapter 4

Unintentional Techniques of Self-deception

'For one thing is needful; that a human being attain his satisfaction with himself ... only then is a human being at all tolerable to behold.'

Nietzsche

Having established that self-deception is best understood using the third approach to the two-person model, we need to examine through what means it occurs. Much recent philosophical work on self-deception has looked at the characteristic techniques and strategies that people use to become self-deceived. In the next two chapters, both intentional and unintentional strategies for becoming self-deceived will be identified and examined. Once this question has been settled, we will be in a better position to solve the paradoxes mentioned at the outset.

Firstly, this chapter will examine some recent experimental evidence suggesting that self-deception can be caused through unintentional but motivated processes of belief biasing. The evidence suggests that there are causal mechanisms which can alter our beliefs but which are not triggered intentionally.

The tropistic model: A tropism is the involuntary directed movement or orientation of a plant in response to an external stimulus. Tropisms can be classified according to the external stimulus acting on the plant. There are thus phototropisms (responses to light), gravitropisms (responses to gravity), hydrotropisms (responses to water) and thigmotropisms (responses to touch). Plants will have a strong tendency to turn towards the light and away from gravity. The essential point is that in response to any such impetus a plant will respond blindly, causally and automatically.

The application of this botanical term is useful in a mentalistic setting. For unintentionally caused self-deception occurs when automatic and unintentional mechanisms cause one's belief-acquisition processes to be biased towards a favoured belief. The most basic example of a mental trope is that of wishful thinking, where a desire for p leads by a process of sheer causality to a belief that p. In the tropistic model of self-deception, the desire for p to be the case tropistically leads to the desire to believe that p. Nonetheless, the analogy cannot be stretched too far. Tropisms do not operate through motivation, and exist in the category of blind forces. Motivational forces must prime a person's cognitive machinery before he or she is self-deceived.

Johnston's theory of self-deception: One leading theorist who makes use of the tropism idea is Mark Johnston. According to Johnston, the paradoxes of self-deception occur because we overrationalise mental processes that are purposive but unintentional. For Johnston, homuncular explanations multiply subagents unnecessarily, each 'with their own interests and action plans'.[30] His main claim in response to Pears is that the lapse into homuncularism is a 'premature response to the surface paradox of self-deception'.[31] This is because it is thought that self-deception, to live up to its name, must be a fully fledged

52

intentional process that involves a deceiving and deceived mental part, based on the two-person model. He thinks that the surface paradoxes of self-deception show that it could not be represented as a conscious, intentional act of lying to oneself. Self-deception instead involves:

> ... processes that serve some interests of the self-deceiver, processes whose existence within the self-deceiver's psychic economy depends upon this fact, but processes that are not necessarily initiated by the self-deceiver for the sake of those interests...[32]

We can see how he arrives at this idea by tracing his exposition of wishful thinking. He believes that self-deception is a species of wishful thought. Wishful thinking is similar to self-deception in that it points to motivated belief that is not responsive to any available evidence. It differs from self-deception in that the self-deceiver accepts a proposition against what he recognises to be the implications of the evidence. He says that it would be highly suspect to come to believe intentionally some proposition p while recognising that one does not nor will not come to possess evidence for it. He argues that 'nothing could be an intentional act of immediately coming to wishfully believe in the recognised absence of supporting evidence.'[33]*

Johnston suggests that we should understand wishful thought not as the outcome of any rational process in the mind, but as the result of a desire for p and an anxious fear that not p, between them which cause the belief that p. It is not the result of practical reasoning occurring in the unconscious. Instead, it is a mental mechanism or

---

*What the author means is that we could never intentionally engage in wishful thinking.

tropism by which a desire that p and accompanying anxiety that not p set the conditions for the rewarding response of coming to believe that p.

Johnston illustrates this idea with the example of an anxiety-beset gambler. A non-superstitious gambler playing blackjack has hopeful fantasies of getting blackjack on his next hand. He does not believe these fantasies and would not act on them by increasing his bets if his first card was an ace. His desire to be dealt blackjack gives him no reason to believe that he will and he has no interest in the consequences of belief for his future doxastic states. His getting lost in his fantasy is not an intentional act. According to Johnston:

> A future tensed belief (e.g. that blackjack is expected) can reduce anxiety about the future. If this is the rewarding role of anticipatory wishful thought – the reduction of anxiety about a desired outcome – then we should expect anticipatory wishful thought in the presence of the desire that p coupled with the fear that not p.[34]

Wishful thinking is unintentional. For if it were interpreted otherwise, it would be difficult to see how one could adopt an attitude that one recognised as not in any way reflecting the way the world truly is. Wishful thinking is not rationalisable or intentional, but does carry out a purpose in helping to reduce one's anxiety about a given state of affairs.

While wishful thinking does not necessitate a division of the mind, things are different with self-deception. The self-deceiver adopts the wishful belief despite at some level recognising contradictory evidence. Anxiety cannot be reduced if a wishful belief is 'copresent in consciousness'[35] with a belief or acknowledgement of counter-evidence. Somehow the subject must cease consciously recognising that the evidence contradicts his belief. The paradoxes arise when we consider how the individual accomplishes this. The strategy to rid oneself of a recognition of something suggests a censor who actively shields information from the conscious mind. Such a censor cannot be the main conscious system, because then we are confronted by a paradox: the main system would have to aim to bury the anxiety-producing belief in order to forget it.

Johnston believes that the way out of this paradox of censorship is the same as the escape route from the paradox of wishful thinking. The burial of material via repression should be regarded as a tropistic and purposive but also unintentional operation. It operates for the purpose of reducing anxiety by ridding the conscious self of its awareness of material or by disguising material that would, under other circumstances, lead the individual to form an unpleasant belief. It is not 'an intentional act of some subagency guided by its awareness of its desire to forget'.[36] Johnston's theory therefore dispenses with the need for the Pearsian model. He can interpret self-deception as a motivated but unintentional phenomenon.

Some aspects of Johnston's theory are similar to mine. In order to compare our theories, it is best to set out the conditions for entering self-deception that Johnston might offer. We appear to have at least the following 5 conditions:

i) Jones is aware of evidence suggesting p and believes p.
ii) Jones becomes anxious at p.
iii) Jones has a subsequent anxious desire for not p.
iv) Jones has a subsequent anxious desire to believe not p
v) The anxious desire to believe not p causes tropistically the burial of Jones' unwanted belief and the promotion of the belief not p.

55

Condition i, the notion of a person being aware of and believing some evidence, appears in Johnston's account and is similar to my own condition i. Condition iii introduces the notion of a 'core desire', while condition iv appears to mirror the biasing desire. A slight difference that could be mentioned is that desire need not be motivated by a preceding anxious state. Anxiety is but one possible emotional state found in self-deception. The major point of disagreement concerns the exclusive emphasis on the cause of self-deception. Johnston assumes that the sole type of generating cause is tropistic. I argue that there can be an intentional causal structure, as well as a tropistic one. I have left this critique of Johnston until later.

We have looked at a conceptual analysis of self-deception in terms of tropistic causation. It is time now to take stock of some recent empirical findings suggesting that humans are capable of deceiving themselves via tropistic or unintentional means.

Much recent work in cognitive psychology has focused on the psychological defences we erect in the face of threatening or anxiety-provoking information. This work has been thought to give some experimental underpinning to the idea of self-deception.

The notion of perceptual defence is based around the idea that what we perceive, far from constituting the raw or primary data of experience, is influenced by or based upon our needs, wishes or defences. In numerous laboratory experiments, subjects would be presented with a word for a very brief exposure time, and were then required to state what the presented word was. Exposure times to these words would vary, depending on the subjects being given a long enough period of time to state each one. The studies showed that the subjects took longer to identify words which were obscene, threatening or anxiety-provoking than they did neutral words. The experiments also monitored their heightened galvanic skin responses, by which emotion can be measured.

A natural objection was raised against the results of this work. The experiments did not clearly distinguish between, on the one hand, actual unconscious perceptual defence and, on the other hand, 'conscious response inhibition'. The latter would prevent the subject from reporting the dirty word out of natural embarrassment. Naturally, if the latter was the case, then such studies suggest that subjects refused to divulge what they explicitly knew to their experimenters, something that is disanalogous to self-deception. As this ambiguity has remained unresolved, the idea of perceptual defence cannot really be used as experimental evidence for self-deception.

Another intriguing idea is the notion of 'cognitive schemas'. Schemas constitute the inbred and subliminal rules and expectations which guide our perception of reality, through the use of which we are prepared to comprehend the world in specific ways. The world is fitted, in our perceptions, to how we expect it to be. Many of the perceptual illusions we encounter seem to be based around the idea that reality has an inferential quality; it is not a given. Gilbert and Cooper, in their article 'Social Psychological Strategies of Self Deception', give one such imaginary example:

> ... when we see a dark, shadowy object atop the mantelpiece in our ill-lit study, we know that it is our old-fashioned clock, not a cat. This knowledge enables us to see the long, thin strand that hangs over the edge as an electrical cord, not a tail, and the triangular protrusions at the top as carved figurines rather than ears. This perception, born of expectation, is so compelling and complete that we are quite startled to see the 'clock' spring from the mantelpiece and

begin preening itself on the Oriental rug – until we remember that the clock is away for repair and the cat is not.[37]

It has been thought by some authors that the self could be included as a schema concept. Applying the idea of cognitive schemas to the 'self' concept that each of us possesses, we can say that our beliefs about our own selves, and the fundamental projects that we value, can alter our perceptions of the world in quite radical ways. A self-schema, in other words, can help to verify what we think and value about ourselves by altering our perceptions in desired ways.

Two psychologists, Swann and Read, carried out a study to test the hypothesis that people not only possessed positive and stable self-conceptions but verified them through social interaction. In an initial study, subjects who were classified as either 'self-likers' or 'self-dislikers', were led to believe that a future interaction partner probably, but not certainly, held a favourable expectancy about them. Subjects were later given an opportunity to study the future partner's evaluation of the subject, which was based on the subject's reported attitudes and values. In reality, the interaction partner was entirely fictitious. Subjects, however, were actually given an evaluation containing both positive and negative items, each on a separate slide.

As Gilbert and Cooper state, Swann and Read, after studying the length of time each subject spent considering the evaluation, discovered the following:

> ...self-dislikers spent far more time studying the evaluation of the partner whom they suspected disliked them, whereas self-likers spent more time considering the evaluation of the partner whom they suspected liked them ... people spent more time considering

58

information from sources whom they thought would confirm rather than disconfirm their self-conceptions.

Such self-schemas work 'by drawing attention to selected aspects of the feedback we receive, filling in gaps with self-enhancing information, or by assimilating ambiguous information to a positive self-conception'.[38] There is no need to interpret the variation in time spent in the evaluation as an intentional act. In order to preserve a self-conception, one may deceive oneself by varying the amount of time one spends looking at information. These subjects spent a greater amount of time looking at and encoding 'positive' information that confirmed their self-conceptions, even at the expense of other, contradictory data. The degree of time spent evaluating information may be based on one's pleasure and interest in the data perceived. It need not reflect a belief that the best way to present oneself with positive-hypothesis-confirming data is to focus on such data, or to neglect contrary data. The variation in the level of attention does not therefore have to be interpreted as being part of any intentional strategy.

In another study, Ziva Kunda defends the view that motivation can influence 'the generation and evaluation of hypotheses, of inference rules, and of evidence', and that motivationally biased memory search will result in 'the formation of additional biased beliefs and theories that are constructed so as to justify desired conclusions'.[39]

In one study, a group of undergraduate students, 75 women and 86 men, read an article alleging that 'women were endangered by caffeine and were strongly advised to avoid caffeine in any form'. One prominent danger cited in the article was that excessive coffee drinking could contribute to fibrocystic disease and the onset of breast cancer. The subjects were then all asked how convinced they were that there was a strong connection between caffeine and fibrocystic disease. The males were more convinced than the female heavy consumers, and there was very little difference in conviction between the heavy and light male caffeine consumers. Among the females, however, heavy consumers of coffee were much less convinced of the connections between the two than were light consumers. The crucial factor in the different evaluations and inferences appeared to be the personal motives of the individuals concerned. According to Kunda, the lower level of support showed by the heavy caffeine-drinking females was due to 'motivational processes designed to preserve optimism about their future health'[40]

Let us apply the conditions for entering self-deception in the Kunda experiment. A female coffee drinker encounters evidence that clearly supports the belief that she is risking her health. She is aware of this evidence and the belief it leads to and cannot help accepting it. At the same time, she enjoys a pursuit, namely drinking coffee. The clash that can lead to self-deception arises out of the discrepancy between what she desires to believe is true of herself (a person who does not indulge in a dangerous pursuit) and a threatening belief (she is endangering herself). So she believes a proposition p on the basis of evidence e (coffee is threatening) but desires not p (that coffee is not threatening to health). The latter is the core desire. This leads to a desire to believe she is not drinking something that is threatening her health.

It appears that there are unintentional (tropistic) means of altering the data that have been presented. One plausible way of biasing beliefs in this scenario is to vary the amount of time spent attending to evidence. The heavy coffee drinker pays selective attention to the evidence and will vary the amount of time assessing it depending on whether a given part tallies with what she desires to believe. As a result, the overall evidence is favourably represented to her. As with the Swann and Read experiment, we do not need to interpret the variation in time as an intentional strategy.

Nisbett/Ross: Nisbett and Ross, in their volume *Human Inference: strategies and shortcomings of social judgement*, make a number of claims about the unconscious cognitive sources of irrationality. The authors outline a number of the most frequent inferential errors in human judgement but stress the non-motivated nature of such errors. They describe these erroneous processes as the 'almost inevitable products of information-processing strategies',[41] and make no claims about the nature of self-deception. I will outline the four main cognitive biases that the authors cite:

VIVIDNESS OF INFORMATION: People's inferences and behaviour 'are so much more influenced by vivid, concrete information than by pallid and abstract propositions of ... greater ... evidential value'.[42] The vividness of a specific datum is described in terms of three factors:

i) <u>Its degree of emotional interest</u>. Among the set of factors determining one's emotional interest in an event, they cite the following: the nature of one's acquaintance with participants in an event, the hedonic relevance of the event and the consequences of the event, for the participants.

ii) <u>Its concrete and imagery-provoking nature</u>. Factors of concreteness include the 'degree of detail and specificity about actors, actions and situational context'.[43]

iii) <u>Its proximity to the individual in terms of sensory, temporal and spatial properties</u>. Basically, vivid information 'is more likely to be stored and remembered than pallid information is'.[44] It is precisely because information is more easily stored and remembered that it will be more likely to be retrieved at a later date, thereby affecting our subsequent inferences and exerting a disproportionate influence on our beliefs.

According to Nisbett and Ross, one of the most important causes of information becoming salient is due to one's emotional interest in that information or its degree of emotional impact. In their original presentation of the bias, the authors say that a given event can have a greater or lesser emotional interest depending very much on the 'nature of one's acquaintance with the participants in the event'. Events that happen to us, 'are more interesting for perhaps no other reason than it is to us that they are happening.' Nisbett and Ross also say that the emotional interest of information will be influenced by the 'participants' needs, desires, motives and values'.[45]

In their original presentation of the bias, the authors cite one's emotional interest in and affective stance towards events and the participants in them. They give as an example, the different factors determining the extent or lack of vividness of information for a hearer when he is told about an unlucky car crash. The most important factors are the hearer's knowledge of the participants and his affective stance or attitude towards them. If the hearer has a personal relationship to the actors in the event, then information about what happens in that event will be more salient to him.

Nisbett and Ross stress in particular that the use of this bias is generally automatic, non-reflexive, and also non-intentional.

THE AVAILABILITY HEURISTIC: According to the

authors, when people are required to 'judge the relative frequency of objects', people may 'often ... be influenced by the availability of the objects or events, that is, their accessibility in the processes of perception, memory or construction from imagination'.[46] To take an example, a subject may come to believe that there are more words beginning with 'r' than having 'r' in the third position, because the former are much easier to remember. In fact, the latter are far more numerous.

THE CONFIRMATION BIAS: During the testing of a particular hypothesis, people will tend to search more for confirming than for contrary data, even when one's hypothesis is a tentative one. A great deal of what Nisbett and Ross have in mind is the persistence with which hypotheses are maintained despite their evidential discrediting. Subjects tend to persevere in their beliefs 'beyond the point at which the evidence can sustain them', and lack 'the ability to intervene and test hypotheses by generating new data'.[47]

The characteristics of the confirmation bias are that 'impressions formed on the basis of early evidence survive exposure to inconsistent evidence presented later, and beliefs survive the total discrediting of their evidence base'.[48] When such beliefs are challenged, people use 'cognitive machinery' in order to discredit 'uncongenial evidence and to bolster supportive evidence'.[49] Among the cognitive mechanisms that they discuss are a variety of encoding and decoding biases that favour confirmation of prior hypotheses or beliefs over disconfirmation. Evidence is cited which supports the idea that people tend to 'recognise the relevance of confirming cases more readily than contrary evidence and therefore tend to search for such cases in evaluating their hypotheses'.[50]

One specific cause of this belief perseverance is the

desire to believe something. Given an individual's emotional commitment to a given belief, he will sustain it by 'whatever cognitive tricks are necessary'. While Nisbett and Ross prefer information-processing explanations for perseverance phenomena, they acknowledge that these may often be triggered 'by purely motivational considerations'.[51]

TENDENCY TO SEARCH FOR CAUSAL EXPLANATIONS: People tend to search for causal explanations of the world, and, while this is not in itself irrational, these can be very ill-founded in certain circumstances. Nisbett and Ross, in particular, make note of subjects' tendency to generate erroneous or superfluous causal explanations of events in experimental situations.

These inappropriate treatments of data constitute a means by which our belief states may become altered through skews and biases. If we regard these processes as unmotivated, they cannot feature in an explanation of self-deception. For they would then be blind non-rational forces working to disrupt the mind, and we have already noted the importance of motivation in the causation of self-deception. It does not take a massive stretch of the imagination to see how motivated self-deception and belief distortion can be aided by the operation of such mechanisms. In other words, we can see how a person's desire to believe that something is the case could tropistically lead to the operation of the above mechanisms.

The salience principle: A simple idea, which I have termed 'the salience principle of desire', will help us better understand the application of these mechanisms. If a subject has an anxious, fearful or 'hungry' desire for a proposition to be true, the object of that desire will become more salient to the subject, even to the extent of appearing in unwarranted contexts. If a man wants an object enough,

64

that object can become far more salient for him, as when he strongly desires food and any food (or object resembling food) is rendered much more vivid. A man in a desert, desperate for water, will seem to see water where it is not; he will be subject to the deluding hope of hallucinatory mirages. The pseudoscientist, desperate for his theory to be true, may begin to see confirmation of his ideas more readily than a neutral observer. In searching for a historical explanation of the cause of the Boer War, I find data pertinent to the subject. The ideals of correct inference in historical research dictate an objective consideration of the total available evidence I possess. Instead, I find my attention shifting and latching onto an explanation that I previously believed was original and satisfactory. Soon I may build this interpretation into everything I read. Desire that is hungry enough will affect an individual's inferential judgement by rendering an object disproportionately vivid.

None of these biases or processes require a Pearsian subagent to direct them, and none of them call for homuncular explanation. They are unintentional because the agent does not possess any relevant beliefs about how to increase the salience of data or how adequately to manipulate it. These biases give backing to the claim that self-deception can arise out of a structure of motivated self-misrepresentation which is not initiated for that reason by an individual.

Let us look more specifically at how we could apply the Nisbett/Ross mechanisms in a putative case of self-deception. I will concentrate on the first three mechanisms only.

VIVIDNESS OF INFORMATION: There are at least three ways in which information can take on an enhanced salience, the first being one's emotional interest in the information obtained.

The glutton already has a clear emotional stake in the problematic question of gluttony. This is because she is both the subject and object of her questioning and has an emotional commitment to questions about her identity. She can easily make accurate diagnoses of the gluttonous habits of other people to whom she bears little emotional relation. In her own case, detached objectivity is impossible, and, moreover, she possesses a clear motive for misrepresenting data about her gluttonous habits. Similarly, the lady in our earlier example could tell a female friend, without any hesitation, that her husband was guilty of being an adulterer on account of his suspicious behaviour. She would be unable, however, to admit this in her own case. Clear irrationality is manifested in this behavioural discrepancy.

The information the glutton obtains can be more or less vivid in terms of its concreteness and also by its tendency to prompt sensory imagery. Suppose the glutton is weighing up the evidence for whether she has recently become a glutton. She looks in her diary at some lunch appointments and comes across two very different entries:

23.03 Lunch appointment: Business meeting at Ritz. Huge delicious meal: meats, bread, wine, cakes, exotic delicacies.
28.03 Business lunch, 12.45 at 34 Pimlico Sq. Light tuna salad.

The first of these two represents evidence for the unfavoured belief that she is (or was) a glutton. Clearly she would prefer that this entry had not been written and that she could now suppress it. Now, we may well ask just how the glutton can unintentionally overlook or fail to take into account such clear 'negative' evidence. Firstly, she has to recognise that this part of the evidence poses a threat to her. Secondly, she has to use an intentional strategy to bury the evidence. This problem need not arise at all.

The second entry is far more desirable for her self-image and prima facie constitutes good evidence for her more modest eating habits. If her motivation is to believe that she is not a glutton, then any information or evidence which invokes desirable images will become more vivid and salient in her mind. The fact that the second diary entry becomes more vivid makes it more likely to become the focus of her immediate attention and also to appear in her mind as a stronger form of evidence for her chosen hypothesis. The resulting vividness of this evidence, which is due to its added concreteness, will render it easier to recall in memory and will therefore affect her subsequent judgement.

It is important to realise that the workings of this bias do not admit of an intentional explanation. The cognitive mechanisms do not operate by appealing to the glutton's beliefs about how she might bias data to acquire a favoured belief. They are unintentional because she lacks any relevant beliefs about how to increase the salience of some data or how adequately to manipulate it.

AVAILABILITY HEURISTIC: The availability heuristic is clearly also working here. When the glutton tries to recall some of the evidence for her past eating habits, it will be much easier for her to remember instances of dieting, fasting or modest eating. This is because these memories accord with what she is happy to remember as a result of the previous bias. Under the influence of the availability heuristic, the glutton will then infer that those instances have therefore been more frequent than she has previously thought.

Naturally, the objective frequency of instances of gluttony

in her mind is not indicated by how much she's able to remember. She has had her belief-acquisition processes skewed because she is not being allowed to take into account a wider range of data that would suggest a less favoured belief. The vividness of information in her mind is an inefficient guide to its evidential value. Hence the salience and concreteness of some of her favoured memories gives her a defective appreciation of reality.

As before, there is no intentional activity here. The subject lacks a belief that the best way to discard the rational belief (I am a glutton) and promote another is to search in a specific way in her memory for certain items. These items automatically come to her recollection with varying degrees of ease.

CONFIRMATION BIAS: Initially, the glutton's anxious desire not to be a glutton constitutes a powerful and unyielding emotional commitment. This could lead her unintentionally to see a very dubious confirmation of her favoured belief in all encounters with relevant data. In her hypothesis evaluation, the glutton does not adopt a neutral standpoint towards her available evidence. Driven by a desire to confirm her cherished belief, she overlooks negative evidence and views as 'relevant' more favourable data. One suggestion from the Swann and Read study is that one main factor that determines the weight given to data is the amount of time spent analysing it. In regard to the diary entries, the glutton could be so fixated on positive evidence for the favoured belief that she ends up believing it has disproportionately high value as data. The biasing desire draws the glutton's mind to a selective appraisal of evidence and does not allow equally relevant negative evidence to count in her assessment. The cognitive machinery that allows this to occur can be judged to be driven by motivational considerations.

Let us summarise what is happening when these mechanisms are triggered and how this relates to the structure of self-deception outlined in chapter 3.

Image Preservation: The glutton's primary motivation is the preservation of a positive self-image. 'Being gluttonous' to her represents a thoroughly negative self-image, one that threatens to overwhelm her sense of value and self-worth. She dislikes gluttony and desires to be in the category of non-gluttons.

Unfavoured Belief Acquired: The lady nonetheless initially strongly suspects and then believes that she is a glutton on the basis of her memories of her overindulgent eating habits, her numerous recollections of cookbooks in her home and her colleagues' remarks.

Core And Biasing Desire: This produces a clash of propositional attitudes forcing an internal conflict within her. Her desire to be a non-glutton and her wish to promote the corresponding belief goes against her available evidence, beliefs and the total-evidence principle.

Data/Evidential Manipulation: At this stage we can hypothesise that the core and biasing desires, together with an anxious belief about what she believes to be true, causally trigger off the biases we have just discussed. But whereas Nisbett and Ross picture these biases in purely cognitive terms, we can now see how a subject's desires could lead to a *motivated* structure of self-misrepresentation quite characteristic of self-deception.

We have preserved the three features of the two-person model here, without resorting to a Pearsian subagent inside her head. None of these processes require a Pearsian subagent to direct them and none of them call for homuncular explanation. Such cognitive biases afford a wonderfully convenient way of misrepresenting data that would otherwise conflict with a desired perception of reality.

Chapter 5

Intentional Techniques of Self-deception

'Beaucoup d'hommes ont un orgueil qui les pousse à cacher leurs combats et à ne se montrer que victorieux.'

Balzac

The previous chapter outlined the ways in which people could deceive themselves by motivated but unintentional means. More often than not, people deceive themselves intentionally and with a marked degree of deliberation. The lovestruck lady knows that if she does not walk past the cafe, she will avoid confronting the deceitfulness of her partner and will thus help promote the belief that he is faithful. The glutton deliberately refuses to assess some of her diary evidence for fear that it will confirm her gluttonous past. In both cases, they act intentionally so as to achieve their preferences or goals. Intentional self-misrepresentation occurs when people deceive themselves by intentionally using various strategies of evidential manipulation.

Intentional self-deception is self-deception performed for a reason. The distinction between intentional and tropistic causation centres around whether or not an agent's actions, utterances and beliefs follow a logical and rationally ordered sequence. This partly involves a degree of knowledge

71

concerning the way in which one's actions are related to one's goals, although this knowledge may be tacit.

The first connotation of the term 'intention' stresses a degree of knowledge, planning and self-awareness that an individual inputs into his future acts. An intention is usually thought of as an attitude that one has to one's actions in the future, a characteristic and conscious plan to act in a given way in accordance with a goal. An intention to x can be characterised in terms of a fixed commitment that a person makes to try and bring x about. If one's action is intentional in this sense one would usually be able to specify why one is acting in a particular way, because intentional commitments involve a heavy degree of reflection and deliberateness. As one cannot accidentally be planning to act in a given way in the future, so too one should be able to specify what one is intentionally doing now or what one's prior intention was. It may take a certain amount of probing or reflection, but the correct answer is always supposed to emerge.

An intention can also be conceived in terms of a structure of practical reasoning, although not one that the agent is necessarily aware of at any one time. Actions are performed with an intention or are classified as being intentional when they exhibit the following structure:

i) A desires to believe p.
ii) A believes that if he performs strategy x, he will believe p.
iii) A therefore desires to perform strategy x.

The point I stress is that the agent need not be aware at all times of the logical and rational sequences inherent in his activities. He may not at all times be able to state what it is that he intends to do or what intentional projects he is engaged in. In other words, there are such things as

72

tacit or hidden intentions in which agents are capable of being mistaken about their motives. This leads to the 'two factor' theory of intentions.

Among the intentional techniques used by self-deceivers are the following: evasion, overcompensation, selective focus and selective evidence gathering, and, above all, rationalisation. These techniques are essential to an understanding of self-deception.

EVASION: Evasion is a form of attention manipulation in which one deliberately refuses to confront or think about something that is unpleasant or threatening. It is an avoidance technique, enabling one to avoid contemplating negative and unfavourable evidence and thus maintain an irrational belief state. To illustrate, let us go back to Pears' lovestruck girl. If the girl is asked why she does not want to look at her lover's incriminating diary, she may ignore the question, run out of the room, complain of feeling ill and do everything to avoid thinking about the issue.

Naturally, the girl can only be deliberately evasive about such evidence if she already believes or strongly suspects that it points to something threatening or 'not to be faced'. By evading it, she prevents herself from challenging an established and cherished belief which is vital to her self-esteem. The more she successfully evades this evidence and its hostile implications, the longer she can remain in a deluded and irrational state.

We can set out schematically the intentional structure behind evasion:

i) Girl has evidence suggesting the belief that p.
ii) Girl believes that p.
iii) Girl desires that not p
iv) Girl desires to believe that not p.

73

v) Girl believes that by being evasive she will believe or continue to believe that not p.

vi) Girl therefore desires to be evasive.

Evasion is very much like intentional selective focus. Here one intentionally directs one's attention to those aspects of one's present or past attention (memories) because some are more pleasant to contemplate. The girl in Pears' example may tell herself that it is worthless to consider the evidence for her lover's infidelity because of his previous behaviour and good character. She will therefore intentionally focus on those aspects of their past which confirm this idea and which she finds more pleasing. She will know that by focusing on pleasant memories or thoughts she will thereby lessen the impact of those that are negative and unpleasant.

SELECTIVE EVIDENCE GATHERING: The girl's desire to disbelieve in her lover's infidelity leads her to overlook evidence that she knows it is easy to obtain. She can obtain evidence about her partner's activities from two different sources: a friendly and intelligent colleague who claims to have seen the act of infidelity and her partner's brother, who believes he is the fount of virtue. The sources provide widely divergent opinions and the one she chooses will reflect her existing judgement. When she chooses to visit her partner's brother to obtain favourable evidence, she is really engaging in a secret strategy – the motives for which cannot be spelt out – for bolstering her existing biased judgement.

RATIONALISATION: Rationalisation is the most common technique used by self-deceivers. It is a way of providing an ostensibly reasonable explanation for one's activities, beliefs, emotions or attitudes when these are questioned or appear unjustified. The resulting explanations and justifications are neither accurate nor rational. Rationalisation is at least an attempt to give reasons for what one does or how one thinks, something that betrays a genuine concern for being a reasonable agent. It is therefore an exercise in quasi- or pseudo-rationality which operates against the background of genuine rationality.

The glutton might start to have severe misgivings about her convictions. She might also be aggravated by the reasons she has put forward for thinking she is a modest eater, believing that they might give only weak support for what she thinks. Alternatively, and more commonly, she might have her beliefs directly challenged by other people. A friend might accuse her of ignoring diary evidence, feigning ignorance of her dietary habits, and deliberately neglecting the advice of her doctor to cut out excessive eating. How will she respond? She could start by saying that her doctor has only seen her on a couple of occasions and only briefly mentioned the gluttony issue. She could claim that what her doctor said was only an opinion and that he was likely to be incorrect. She could also add that her diaries only provide selective evidence for what she has eaten, a fact brought to light by the fact that she has made very few entries in it.

These would be classic cases of rationalisation, where one conveniently twists the interpretation of evidence for an unfavoured belief, thereby manipulating one's own better judgement. Two important points need to be made about rationalisations. Firstly, the glutton has attempted to justify her actions, but only after doubts have surfaced about what is really going on in her own head. If she has a permanently settled conviction about something, she needs little reason to bolster it with clever argument or to create reasons for why it is justified.

Secondly, rationalisation can only be used when one's

beliefs can be subject to a degree of interpretative leeway. Thus far, the evidence from the glutton's diary and the regular contents of her larder strongly point to her being gluttonous. If she is thinking rationally, she ought to believe that she is a glutton, but there is still room for a little doubt. In cases, however, where the evidence is overwhelming and there is no room for manoeuvre, one cannot properly deceive oneself. People do not deceive themselves about being hairy or having spots on their face. If someone looks into the mirror and denies what is clearly visible, he may be deranged or deluded, not self-deceived. Rationalisations therefore appear to have at least four essential elements:

i) A rationalisation offers a purported account by a subject of some action x.
ii) It is an account accepted as true by an agent.
iii) It is prima facie a rational account of x.
iv) It offers a false account of x.

In a standard case of rationalisation, the following schema could be constructed:

i) I believe that my action x and promoted belief p is caused by (reason) R (D1 + B1), where D1 and B1 are belief and desire tokens.
ii) Awareness of R gives me discomfort.
iii) I desire that x is caused by R1 (D2 + B2).
iv) I desire to believe x is caused by R1.
v) I believe that by rationalising cause of x, I can believe it was caused by R1.
vi) I desire to rationalise cause of x.
vii) I rationalise cause of x as being due to R1 and thus believe my reason for x is R1 despite believing also that it is caused by R.

76

Rationalisation is clearly an intentional activity. We can detect rational structure in the glutton's decision to provide herself with reasons for acting other than those that truly motivate her. The actual structure of rationalisation is similar to the structure we gave for self-deception at the start. Initially, I believe R is the reason for my xing (condition i). R is the reason I wish to avoid having or believing as my reason for xing (condition ii). Conditions iii and iv play the same role as the core and biasing desires respectively. The latter is represented by the person having a desire to believe that x is caused by R1 rather than R. Conditions v and vi follow the same pattern that we established for intentionally caused self-deception. In condition vii we see the fulfilment of this intention in action. The conditions for the aetiology of self-deceptive rationalisation thus mirror those of core self-deception.

It is helpful to distinguish between rationalisation as used in self-deceptive and non-self-deceptive contexts. An example of the latter occurs in post-hypnotic action. Paula decides to undergo hypnosis and, while under the hypnotist's spell, is ordered to wipe the floor with a paintbrush when she wakes. She is woken and, as soon as she receives a sign, begins to carry out the hypnotist's commands. When asked why she is cleaning the floor, Paula begins to confabulate her reasons for acting in this way. She effectively begins to rationalise her odd behaviour, producing some reasons that have an edge of plausibility but which are not the real basis for her behaviour. The confabulation of reasons for such post-hypnotic behaviour, however, cannot be likened to self-deceptive rationalisation. Quite simply, there is no relevant motive for her not producing another (better) reason, one which would have been more consistent with any available evidence. She has no evidence that she was made to perform an activity via an order implanted by a hypnotist. Furthermore, if she did, it would scarcely cause discomfort. Hence, as a post-hypnotic subject, she lacks a motive to deceive herself.

Mixed Cases: In this chapter, we have concentrated on the ability of agents to intentionally mislead themselves. It is essential to stress that individual cases of self-deception are not the exclusive product of either tropistic or intentional strategies. Even though two types of strategies form, by definition alone, mutually exclusive categories, this should not lead us to think that a particular case of self-deception may not have been the causal product of both types of strategy. Consider the following case:

A man is deeply in love with his wife. He has, however, become increasingly anxious because she has started to arrive home much later than usual. She shows him much less affection than she used to and communicates with him less frequently. She seems distant but is nonetheless happy to talk about other colleagues at work with whom she has formed a closer relationship. He has also been told that she has been seen regularly in the company of one particular male colleague with whom she is on very amicable terms.

The man begins to conjure up clever quasi-rational explanations for the signs of his wife's marital infidelity, knowing that this will help alleviate the stress of believing that his marriage is under threat. He systematically evades the scrutiny of sceptical peers who suspect that his wife is indeed an adulterer. He may choose to avoid some of these peers and, instead, seek the company of his mother-in-law, who does not have a cross word to say about her daughter. While such intentional strategies are clearly being employed, they are not the sole generators of self-deception. He may find images of a happy and tranquil marriage much easier to recollect because they are more vivid or salient. Also, because these memories are easier to recollect, he may assume that there have been more instances of happy than unhappy times in his marital life, a fact that gives him less reason to presume that she is seeking romance elsewhere. The selectiveness of his attention and his biased memory recall subconsciously generate a biased view of the world. Importantly, there are both intentional and tropistic means of biasing relevant data. As Barnes puts it:

> ...there is ... no presumption against a plurality of kinds of mechanism for maximising expected utility. There appear to be in human beings all sorts of non-intentional physiological and psychological mechanisms which have the tendency to maximise expected utility, coexisting with the intentional mechanism that has that tendency vis-à-vis rational action.[52]

What is the empirical justification for the description of any particular case? I think it must depend on an interpretation of behavioural data. If there are signs of a structure of intention and of logical reasoning in the subject's action, i.e. if the subject's behaviour exhibits an intelligent rational structure, then we have good grounds for thinking that the person is intentionally self-deceived. We may easily observe the subject and decide that there is no such manifestation of intentional activity. A case involving both types of strategy i.e. involving both a selective amount of assessment time and a rationalisation of the relevant evidence, may prompt us to think in terms of a mixed case of self-deception.

We have looked at both intentional and unintentional mechanisms of belief distortion and self-misrepresentation. We can put these into four main categories:

i) **Biased weighting of favourable evidence:** Under this bias, a small amount of evidence for a favoured belief is given disproportionate and exaggerated weight. Instead of examining the totality of one's available evidence, a small amount of evidence is magnified in importance in order to fit in with what one desires to believe. All of the Nisbett/Ross mechanisms operate under this bias. This bias also manifests itself in the behaviour of some of the subjects in the cognitive experiments from chapter 4. Subjects in the Swann and Read experiments consider information from sources which they think will confirm rather than contradict their self-conceptions. Different levels of attention are paid to the two different sources of evidence, depending on whether or not the information from the source is consistent with the subject's self-conception.

ii) **Biased interpretation of unfavourable data:** Here, we actually confront unfavoured data, whether it relates to our thoughts, emotions, beliefs or some element of external reality. By a process of skewed reasoning, we then interpret it as not counting against a favoured belief. Rationalisation is the clearest case of this strategy.

iii) **Biased avoidance of unfavourable data:** Here, people simply refuse to engage with the unfavourable data. They turn their attention away and concentrate on something else to avoid contemplation. Naturally, evasion is a key strategy here, for this allows subjects to manipulate their attention in such a way that the negative evidence is never considered as such. Under the intentional strategy of selective focus, one similarly focuses on less unfavourable data.

iv) **Biased choice of source material:** This covers the intentional strategy of selective evidence gathering. If one investigates a hypothesis, one needs to choose one's informational sources with great care. This must include assessing the relative likelihood of bias and prejudice in the source and the limitations it brings. In the first case, the informational source one self-deceptively chooses is not selected impartially but with a view to bolstering an existing judgement.

The next chapter will deal with how we overcome the paradoxes we mentioned at the start.

Chapter 6

Coherence Regained – Overcoming Paradox

'View yourself in the deceiving mirror of self-love.'

Philip Massinger

In this chapter, we will see how the paradox of belief and the strategy paradox can be solved without a radical remodelling of the mind. Self-deception in my model can be understood without violating our commonsense notions of mental unity and agency and fragmenting the person into a multiplicity of selves. At the same time, we do not need to alter the characteristics of the phenomenon we are looking at. This model therefore attempts to steer between the philosophical Scylla and Charybdis that plagued the theories of chapters 2 and 3. The crucial claim I will make here is that the notion of mental distance involving a weak rather than strong notion of partitioning can solve both paradoxes of self-deception.

Paradox of Belief: The paradox of belief involved an agent simultaneously holding contradictory beliefs subject to motivational bias. The agent, when self-deceived in believing p, will consciously avow that p, expressing an epistemically irrational belief. Despite this, there are signs that the unfavoured rational belief is accepted at some level by the agent. The lady does not pass by the cafe for fear of witnessing her partner's cheating behaviour. The glutton refuses to scrutinise her cookbooks and diaries. This behaviour can be interpreted in terms of their accepting deep down a belief that they cannot avow. This explains condition vi in chapter 3. This condition was: 'The retention of the new belief, in the face of strong evidence contrary to it, suggests the presence of the rational but unwelcome belief. This belief is still held at some level by the subject but he does not fully spell it out or avow it. It can be detected later in behaviour.'

Aside from any logical difficulties, there is a problem here. If we said that a subject accepted evidence for p, believed a proposition p, and also deliberately asserted a contrary belief, we would have great difficulty in interpreting the person as self-deceived. For it would imply that we could point out to him the evidence for p, gain his assent to it and make him see that it was in his best interests as an epistemic agent to believe p. Despite this, he would still assent to not p for no good reason. Given these conditions, we might be tempted to think of him as delirious or delusional but not as self-deceived.

The self-deceiver, upon interrogation, also sincerely denies that the evidence points to the undesired belief. One condition we must add is that the person's undesired belief that p is motivationally largely inaccessible to him at the time he is self-deceived in believing not p. In order to bring out the full force of this idea, we have to accept a picture of the mind as weakly partitioned.

It would help at this point to introduce the work of Donald Davidson. Davidson believed that in typical cases of self-deception, there is 'something inconsistent by the standards of the agent himself'. The inconsistency will be due primarily to the fact that a person 'believes both a certain proposition and its negation', and to the fact that 'one belief sustains the other'.[53] Davidson asks how one belief could causally sustain a contrary belief, one to which it bore a causal rather than rational relation. In order to accommodate this with his theory of mind, he needs to employ partition in such a way that 'the breakdown of reason relations defines the boundary of a sub-division'.[54]

Davidson assumes the mind can be divided into quasi-independent structures or partitions. These are akin to weak partitions. The partitioning of the mind necessitates that a 'part of the mind must show a larger degree of consistency or rationality than is attributed to the whole'. The whole will obviously be less coherent because of the conflicting beliefs and attitudes of the agent. Each of the two interacting parts of the mind is characterised by there being 'a supporting structure of reasons, of interlocking beliefs, expectations, assumptions, attitudes and desires'. Within each of the elements there must be 'a fair degree of consistency, and where one element can operate on another in the modality of non-rational causality'.[55] This constellation of beliefs and desires allows us 'to characterize certain events as having a goal or an intention'. Essentially we must conceive of the thoughts, feelings and desires of the person as 'interacting to produce consequences on the principles of intentional action, these consequences then serving as causes, but not reasons, for further mental events'.[56] From Davidson's notion of partitioning, I borrow the ideas of mental distance via segregated sets of propositional attitudes.[57]

Disavowal: The key to a self-deceiver sustaining contrary beliefs is that both beliefs are not simultaneously avowed. While one is fully and explicitly committed to the promoted belief, the nagging buried belief, together with the belief in the operation of the biasing desire (the cautionary belief as

Pears calls it), is at the same time inaccessible. I take an accessible belief to be a mental state that is available to the subject, one that can be manifested and expressed in characteristic ways, i.e. in thought and speech, and one that the subject has an immediate awareness of. An inaccessible belief does not meet these conditions. There is a further existential condition. An accessible belief has to be one that the individual somehow explicitly avows.

As Fingarette would say, the unfavoured belief is not one that can be fully 'spelt out' by the agent during self-deception. To spell out a belief is to be able to acknowledge that belief without shame or anxiety. It is to fully identify with the belief as one's own and to accept without difficulty the full entailments of that belief. The normal language of avowal is closely connected to the notion of identity. Avowal is an inner act in which one identifies oneself with an engagement, commitment or action. Those things take on a personal quality which one accepts as fundamental to one's identity.

The act of avowal signifies personal acceptance of something that comes, as it were, from the heart. This is more than simply understanding a self-referential fact. I may be born in France but never accept that I am a Frenchman. Taken as a belief about my place of birth and rights of citizenship, the statement is plainly false. But taken as an expression of a disavowal of identification, it makes far more sense. I do not identity myself as a Frenchman because it is not an existential or moral commitment that I am happy with. If I avow this identify, it is an existential choice that reflects my philosophical outlook and my personal history; it is who I choose to be as a moral agent.

Disavowal in this sense is a disengagement from certain things that one is closely involved in. The glutton overeats but because this clashes with an existential commitment to seeing herself as attractive, she refuses to acknowledge that what she is doing is overeating. Any unfavourable beliefs or strong suspicions must become inaccessible to that part of her mind which is responsible for self-reflection, avowal and 'spelling out'.

If I cannot accept some information because it not does fit in with my personal commitments and self-image, it has an alien quality. It must be somehow buried or suppressed and cannot be allowed the same explicit recognition that my accessible beliefs have. The self-deceiver, when he glimpses the unfavoured belief, knows there is something 'not to be faced' but cannot bring himself to fully spell out the danger. The beliefs not to be faced need to be hidden away, buried and, in general, kept away from an anxiety-responsive centre of consciousness.

When a belief is inaccessible in the above ways, when it has an alien and 'not me' quality, it becomes separated, or segregated, from the rest of the subject's propositional attitudes. The rational belief, the recognition of evidence for this belief, and the equivalent of the cautionary belief are therefore segregated from one's conscious awareness at the time one is self-deceived in avowing the irrational belief. They have to be partitioned away, pushed away from the store of beliefs, intentions and agent-related dispositions that the person keeps at the forefront of his mind. To solve the paradox of belief, a weak partitive theory of the mind is needed which involves the ideas of inaccessibility and mental distance.

We said at the outset that the paradox involved the possession of two beliefs that had contrary contents and logical entailments, subject to motivational bias. But we have also seen that beliefs can be described or conceived in terms of avowal and acceptance. Two contradictory beliefs can therefore be jointly and simultaneously held by one agent provided they are not both simultaneously avowed, or, as Fingarette would say, spelt out. The beliefs, and corresponding ideas, will not be spelt out fully by the agent when they are unfavourable. But when there is a lack of avowal the rogue beliefs also are pushed away by the agent. To extend the metaphor, some form of motivated mental distance ensures that both beliefs, unfavoured and promoted, are not jointly engaging the attention of the self-deceived agent's attention. When the unfavoured beliefs come to mind, as temporarily they will, mental distance must arise again.

Partition or subagent: The idea of weak partition is a clever metaphor for enabling us to understand a subject who apparently harbours inconsistent attitudes or, as we shall see, an intention of which he is unaware. Partitions do not correspond to a physical divide within the personality. As John Heil puts it, they 'are not to be thought of as permanent mental fixtures'.[58] They are not fully equivalent to the barrier separating consciousness from the unconscious.

The differences between a weak partitive theory of mind and Pears' strongly divisive theory should be clear. A weak partitive theory of mind is acceptable only because it falls short of the agent-divisive ramifications of Pearsian theory. Pears' theory is strongly partitive in that it divides a person into at least two agent-like entities, each with their own intentions and action plans. Subsystems, as strong partitions, are subagents that can act and have reasons of their own. A weak partition is merely a collection of the subject's propositional attitudes that are not logically integrated with another of his sets of attitudes. The same is true of Davidsonian partitions. This is clear when he says that the 'analogy does not have to be carried so far as to demand that we speak of parts of the mind as independent agents'. It is clear that partitions are merely 'constellations of motives', and the 'idea of a quasi-

87

autonomous division is not one that demands a little agent in the division...'[59]

The idea of partitions must be taken metaphorically, as it does not correspond to physical divisions within a single subject's mind. As a result, I claim that my weaker partitive theory makes conceptually less paradoxical claims than that of Pears. Cavell sums up the limitations of the weak subsystemic model in *The Psychoanalytic Mind*:

> The model gives no details about what other beliefs and so on go where; it says nothing about the endurance of substructures over time. Partitioning is a bare logical notion, nothing more. And just this bareness is its virtue. It travels light, requiring no particular theory of psychological development. Yet it can be fitted out with whatever empirical story one thinks is true.[60]

The solution to the strategy paradox: The previous model allows us to understand how mental distance exists between simultaneously held contrary beliefs. We now need to deal with the greater problem, namely how such mental distance comes about. This was the same problem that Pears faced as he regarded the mere fact of mental segregation as a way of restating the facts to be explained. How then can a self-deceiver intend to dupe himself without recognising his intention to do this? We need to recognise that for unintentional self-deception this paradox need not apply, for no intentional states are involved in causing the agent to become self-deceived. Nevertheless, in perhaps the majority of cases the strategy does apply and needs to be faced.

I have continually stressed that the self-deceived agent does not avow some of his or her belief states. They are resultantly segregated from the rest of the agent's avowed

88

and acknowledged mental states. What we must do now is to stress that intentions in self-deception can be similarly desegregated within the agent's mind.

Now, at this stage, we need to recall the two-factor theory of intention. The first way to characterise intentional activity is to see it as based on a fixed commitment to bring about a certain course of action, as when I make a firm intention to go to the gym next week. Here there is a necessary input of awareness, self-conscious reflection and deliberation. When an action is performed intentionally in this sense, one should be able to reflect on what one is doing and why. The second feature of intentional action is that it is characterised by a propositional logical structure in which one's present actions are directly and non-accidentally caused by rationalising beliefs and desires. This is a sufficient condition for an intentional mental state.

The only intelligible way to overcome the strategy paradox is to understand the intentions involved in self-deception in terms of the second but not the first of these features. The solution to the strategy paradox will therefore involve an explanation that cites the subject's intentions being causally efficacious in the production of the promoted and favoured belief without the agent's awareness of them operating in this way. The action is based around strategic motives and intent but these motives are not spelt out or avowed.

In the discussion of the intentional techniques of self-deception, we noted that the glutton cannot represent to herself the true intention with which she was evading, selectively focusing and so on. These motives cannot be spelled out or acknowledged by her and form an engagement that she dissociates herself from. The 'intention to evade' is inaccessible to her and cannot be fully spelt out. That is, she cannot come to an explicit realisation of her true intention to deceive herself. Such intentions are not available to her, as they lack transparency.

I am thinking of a transparent intention as one that I am aware of or one I can explicitly accept as my intention. It is transparent in that I can describe the intention and become aware of its effects in my action and thought. An untransparent intention is one that cannot be explicitly stated, to myself or others, and cannot be consciously believed as my reason for acting.

The distinction between transparent and untransparent intentions contradicts an assumption held by some philosophers that all intentions must be easily spelt out by an agent under probing or analysis. We can call this the 'transparency assumption'. We will see later how Pears' commitment to this assumption leads to his misguided and counter-intuitive proposals for human homunculi.

Let us take, as an example of an intentional self-deceptive technique at work, evasion. We traced a propositional structure for evasion along the following lines:

i) Glutton has evidence suggesting the belief that p.
ii) Glutton believes that p rather than not p.
iii) Glutton desires not p.
iv) Glutton desires to believe not p.
v) Glutton believes that by shifting direction of attention, glutton will believe not p.
vi) Glutton therefore desires to shift attention.

Now, it is clear that the glutton, in the above example, cannot represent her evasiveness to herself as a means of avoiding a threatening belief. Such an explicit train of thought or speech would be absurd. Suppose the glutton's colleague mentions the dreaded topic of her gluttony, and she uncomfortably changes the subject and becomes evasive.

It would make little sense if the glutton produced the following speech:

'You are right to question me. I wish to believe that I am no longer overweight and am not indulging in sumptuous meals. I try therefore to avoid noticing my appointments books, which are full of evidence indicating my gluttony. I do my best to explain away the evidence when I inevitably confront it, and I then suppress my memory of it. I am so good at being evasive in this way that the thought of being a glutton scarcely occurs to me. Please, Joanna, help me to maintain this cognitive state by not mentioning how big I look or how much food there is in the larder.'

Such an explicit rendering of her true intentions is not only risible but absurd. This line of thought would destroy her self-deceptive project, as it would reveal to her that her belief lacked evidential warrant. She would normally strenuously resist any attempt by another person to undermine her basic protected belief (she is not a glutton) by suggesting that it is held because of the desire to ward off anxiety.

It makes more sense to presume that this real motive is hidden, and, in its place, an alternative intention is pronounced. In other words, the glutton resorts to a standard rationalisation for why she has been evasive. The lady might reason that there are better things to talk about, or that she is not in the mood to spend time discussing a trivial matter. A more realistic response might be: 'I don't know what you are talking about. I can't waste time talking about such nonsense. I have lots of food just like anyone else, so I don't need to justify something quite ordinary.' When the evasiveness is pointed out to her, she explains it away. She uses one technique of self-deception

91

(rationalisation) to justify using another (evasion). I call this a 'double structure of self-deception'. Rationalisation keeps one's genuine self-deceptive intention in performing an action inaccessible rather than transparent.

Many philosophers have thought it incoherent to talk of inaccessible intentions. Hampshire, for one, criticises the notion. He believes that intention is a form of knowledge and also that consciousness is inseparable from intention as 'we are always able to answer the question – "What are you doing now?"'.[61] Part of what Hampshire is saying is that an essential element of the structure of intending to do something is that one knows how to do that thing, either directly or indirectly. One cannot be in a mental state of intending to do something without possessing this relevant knowledge. It is possible, however, that we do not need to be aware of this knowledge at all times. We can act intentionally in a rule-governed way, employing various knowledge structures that are tacit, hidden, and reside beneath the realms of reflective awareness. I will briefly look at two philosophical theories that invoke the concept of unconscious intentions in this way, then go on to consider their relevance towards intentions in self-deception.

Rule-following behaviour: Chanowitz and Langer, in their article 'Self-Protection and Self-Inception', highlight the phenomenon of people being sensitive to, yet unaware of, social stimuli. The authors assert that persons act routinely and competently in social situations without explicit reference to the norms that govern their activity in those situations. One example they cite is the automatic and unreflective way in which we respond to traffic signals at a junction. We act routinely every time we are aware of the red light and hence take part in rule-governed social activity. The role in question, however, is acted out without our explicitly spelling out the relevant rules involved. We can be acting intentionally in a given context, yet fail to reflect on the knowledge structures that must exist to give rise to our behaviour patterns. Knowledge of the rules is said to be 'tacit'. This sensitivity requires some degree of knowledge. For without knowing and remembering which procedures are designed to correspond to certain light changes (red – stop), our acting accordingly would be merely a coincidence on a massive scale; it would fail to be intentional. Unless we are asked to provide a justification of our specific manoeuvres, we have only a subliminal and tacit recognition of the rules governing our behaviour.

Grice: A second philosophical theory that requires unconscious intentions is Grice's theory of communication. Grice points out that highly complex intentions are involved in the simple act of communication. These include the intention that the hearer come to believe that p by way of recognising that my saying that p indicates my belief that p, and the intention that you take my believing that p as a reason for you to believe that p. These are unconscious intentions of which the speaker is largely ignorant. While people engaged in communication for thousands of years and lacked the cognitive ability to understand its deeply intentional nature, such intentions nonetheless existed.

Both theories invoke the notion of unconscious intentions. They are, however, of a very different species to self-deceptive intentions. For the above intentions are, as Barnes points out, at least 'non-inferentially recognisable.' This is because a communicator could come to recognise the intentions with which he was credited by Grice, even if these are not spelt out by him during the process of communication. Similarly, we may not spell out our intentions while driving, but we are capable of so doing if asked. In each case, our intentions can, in principle, be recognised. According to Annette Barnes, the following is true of intentions:

> A being has intentions or reasons only insofar as that being can ... ask, and non-inferentially answer, the question 'Why?', where this is taken as a request for one's reason for which, or the intention with which, one does or did so-and-so.[62]

She expresses disquiet at the notion of unconscious 'unrecognisable' intentions. In self-deception, after all, not only can the person not avow our interpretation of his intentional activity but he steadfastly refuses to countenance it. We have already seen why in our discussion of the rationalisation of self-deceiving motives (section on rationalisation in chapter 5). One's true intention in evading, focusing or intending to self-deceive is not spelt out and, because of this, one cannot answer the 'Why' question truthfully. Hence, according to Barnes, one cannot be engaging in intentional activity. Barnes' challenge is to show how the failure of a self-deceiver to answer the 'Why' question shows that this person is still acting intentionally. While the conceptual possibility of *recognisable* unconscious intentions is demonstrated, no light is thrown on those involved in self-deception.

Now, I agree with Barnes that merely by demonstrating the conceptual possibility of unconscious intentions that *can* be recognised, no proof is given of the conceptual possibility of self-deceptive ones. This does not prove that there are no unacknowledged intentions in self-deception. Two points are in order.

Firstly, self-deceivers are guilty of only a temporary epistemic failure. In retrospect, they can quite often detect the motivational and intentional structure behind their previous actions. It is at this later point that agents will often realise the folly of their ways, reflecting on the complex motivational structure in their previous irrational beliefs. The glutton may eventually come to recognise that she really does not have modest eating habits. This may be due to the fact that the evidence is simply too clear-cut to be given a benign interpretation.

Secondly, and more importantly, Barnes ignores the possibility of a hierarchy of self-deceptive intentions, including the intention to hide a relevant intention. In order to be self-deceived about one's having deceived oneself, and in order to misrepresent to oneself one's true reasons for using a method of self-deception (evading), one needs to promote more than one belief. Referring to the glutton, the basic promoted belief is:

p = my belief that 'I am not a glutton'.

In addition, we must assume that a higher-level belief is also promoted:

q = my belief that 'I am not a glutton' is not being sustained by deliberate means of evasion, the result of an unfavourable belief held deep down that I am a glutton nor is it sustained by a deliberate tactic of evasion intended to help me avoid the unfavoured belief.

The glutton deliberately accepts the belief that q, which discounts the view that her belief in non-gluttony is acquired and maintained deliberately because of an unfavourable belief about herself.

The possibility of explaining away the strategy paradox can be met by citing a complex hierarchy of higher-level propositional attitudes: an intention to self-deceive, then an intention to avoid the intention, and possibly an intention to avoid the intention to avoid the intention. That is, while one is in the process of deceiving oneself, i.e. engaging in the evasion and denial illustrated earlier, one cannot explicitly represent the real underlying motive for one's rationalising, evading or denying explicitly to oneself *as* rationalising, evading or denying. I suggested earlier that rationalisation could enable one to engage in an intentional self-deceptive strategy and keep one's intention hidden.

The objection in some quarters is that such a schema could lead effectively to an infinite regress of intentional states, each promoted to serve the last one. I do not think that this is a likely scenario. Naturally, at some point I must realise that I am caused anxiety by one of my threatening beliefs, or I will be unable to intentionally disavow it. In order to then intentionally disavow or misrepresent what I believe, I have to have some knowledge of how to do this. It would scarcely be possible to engage in a strategy of evasion, intentional focus or, particularly, rationalisation, if I knew nothing about the effectiveness of these techniques. In other words, at some level I need to know that they will allow me to avoid an anxious belief state and maintain psychological stability. Acting intentionally in some sense requires knowledge, but this need not be spelt out explicitly. The brief glimpse of what I am doing need not constitute an explicit and full-blown awareness of 'my strategy to deliberately deceive myself'.

Let us go back to the discussion of the glutton's risible speech. Clearly, she is deliberately evasive but she needs to hide this strategy from herself. A lingering and explicit awareness of her real intention might very well destroy her self-deceptive project. Instead of absurdly admitting the effect of her evasive strategy, she rationalises it, pretending that being evasive is justified for other reasons. In other words, she intentionally hides her intentional strategy to deceive herself. We might ask, does she know how to intentionally hide her intentional actions without requiring an intention to hide the intention to hide the intention, i.e. endlessly multiplying intentional states. Bruce Wiltshire makes this suggestion:

> ...out of the corner of the eye we can apprehend an intention in the margin as 'not to be faced squarely' ... it is being apprehended nonverbally in the margin. And the intention to keep the intention in the nonverbalised margin is itself marginal, nonverbalised, unfaced.[63]

Not all intentions need to be so explicitly spelt out; some can be 'marginal' in the way that Wiltshire suggests. The theory is not therefore plagued by the infinite regress problem, and hence I would argue that there is no psychological presumption against a fixed and finite hierarchy of intentional mental states. Fundamentally, the failure to provide coherent accounts of one's intentional activity is also a failure of avowal. The glutton has not spelt out her real intentions or engaged properly with motives that reside deep within her mind.

In both cases, unfavoured beliefs and intentions are not accepted, acknowledged or spelt out by the agent; they must in some sense be separated from those that find favour and satisfaction with the agent. It is the mental-distance story all over again, but not one in which multiple agency is required. We can therefore see a fundamental connection between the solution to each of the paradoxes.

Pears and the transparency assumption: We can see clearly why Pears postulates homuncular mini-agents to direct the process of self-deception. It is because he accepts the transparency assumption that he is forced to postulate subagential causes of intentional activity. For

Pears – assuming the transparency assumption is correct, if a person intentionally deceives himself, the intention behind it must be carried out by an agent (or agential entity) with full awareness of what it intends to do. It is because the main agent (main system) cannot do this, without failing to self-deceive, that another agent (subsystem) is required. This subsystemic agent is alone aware of its own deceptive activity. If we reject the transparency assumption, then we can see how self-deception could be accomplished by one agent. In this way, one can self-deceive intentionally and not be aware of the intentional deception being perpetrated.

Critique of Davidson: Davidson focuses on the intentional acts of the self-deceiver as he feels there are few other ways of accounting for self-deception as a failure of rationality. It is only if an agent intentionally violates his standard or norm of rationality, one which requires him to believe that for which the evidence is most in accord, that we have a case of irrational self-deception. According to Davidson, it is essential that in the explanation of irrationality there is a 'rational element at the core'. This is what creates the paradox of irrationality.

Now, I have assumed that in cases of unintentional self-deception, self-deceivers violate their own standards of rationality, thus demonstrating an inconsistency by their own standards. Self-deceivers may not intentionally manipulate evidence but they are still aware, prior to self-deception, of the weight of contrary evidence against the belief they wish to adopt. They are temporarily aware, while self-deceived, of the belief that they should rationally adopt given their evidence. It is the continuing burial of this rational belief that they are at least partially responsible for. Furthermore, the skewing of their beliefs through cognitive means is something they should recognise.

As such, Davidson neglects to take into account the possibility that there may be unintentional causes of self-deception, and his account is therefore limited to intentional strategies.

Critique of Johnston – the problem of the superintelligent tropes: Johnston's tropistic theory is also inadequate for explaining intentional self-deception. Johnston wants us to believe that his subintentional tropes can account for the full range of self-deceptive behaviour. The tropes are the causal mechanisms that enable an anxious desire for p to lead to an anxiety-reducing belief that p, even in the teeth of opposing evidence. The problem is that the Johnstonian tropes must account for the intentional acts inherent in evasion and rationalisation. Johnston clearly describes these strategies as comprising the core of self-deception and yet describes them as subintentional. That is, he describes the techniques mentioned above as repressive strategies and defines repression as subintentional, i.e. explicitly not guided by reasons. How could we therefore 'tropistically' account for the intentional acts of the self-deceiver – the rationalisations, denials and evasions – given that these techniques seem to require a prior rational structure?

Rationalisation seems to indicate a certain level of guile, contrivance, and clever excuse making. If one was rationalising one's actions and was confronted by the buried belief, then, following Johnston's model, the trope would somehow be required to emit to consciousness some randomly chosen train of thought that would distract the person from a given belief. A mechanical process would have to guide the subject away from one belief supportive of the evidence and, by chance, seize upon a random belief that would suitably provoke less anxiety.

The tropes, however, cannot be required to carry the

burden of intelligent 'work' that is indicated by strategies like rationalisation. By their very nature, tropistic mechanisms operate in a purely blind, mechanical and automatic fashion. They are not mediated by beliefs, which themselves form an integral part of the strategies of intentional self-deception. But successful rationalisation and evasion depends on knowing which beliefs are necessary to alleviate anxiety and maximise expected utility. It is precisely the absence of a belief-desire structure that will ruin any account of apparently intentional processes, ones in which there is more than a characteristic causal connection between a desire for p and a belief that p.

One solution would be to take the whole reasoning process, as we normally encounter it, to be just another application of tropistic activity. According to Johnston, reasoning is blind. All there needs to be for a mental process to be rational is for 'causal relations to hold between mental states one of which is in fact a reason for the other'.[64] He writes:

> First the agent must recognise that he has reasons that support the drawing of a certain conclusion or the performance of an intentional act; second the agent must will the drawing of the conclusion or will the performance of the act; and third, as a result of the willing, draw the conclusion or perform the act. The special something extra distinguishing rational causal processes from the mere mental tropisms that constitute irrational changes in belief is then supposed to be an intervening act of will...[65]

This cannot be right, for, as Johnston says, every time there was a causal connection between someone's recognising that he has reasons to perform an act and his willing the intention to perform the act, there would have to be an intermediate 'willing to will', which would lead us on an infinite regression. In other words, we do not require a homuncular subagent to direct rational thought processes; an agent who sees the rational connection and then wills to draw it. This leaves us with the only credible account of reason:

> ...the case of intentionally drawing the logical conclusion from one's beliefs must ultimately turn on the operation of tropisms connecting the attitudes in question ... we must ... draw some conclusions blindly ... without there occurring in us anything more than an automatic response to those reasons.[66]

Now, this idea strikes me as a little strange. For if all reasoning was purely an automatic, almost conditioned response to one's attitudes, it would seem to give little leeway for differentiating mental from biological causes. Our ability to reason would be rather like a flower turning towards the sun. It would, as Marcia Cavell points out, 'lump the rat's choosing the right door because it has been conditioned to do so with your choosing to give up coffee when the doctor has told you it's the cause of your indigestion'.[67]

Now if this is what Johnston has in mind, then it seems to involve a revised conception of what constitutes mentality. Johnston seems to imply that all reasoning must take place against the background of 'biological or teleological cause'. If this is the proper way to rescue his thesis, then he owes us an explicit account of such a teleological theory of the mental. In the absence of such an account, one can be rightly sceptical about the intellectual manoeuvres involved.

It seems then that the knowledge structures that give rise to techniques of self-deception, such as evasion, rationalisation and selective focus, require a rational structure and explanation. As such, Johnston's account seemingly cannot accommodate a large range of cases of self-deception.

Overall, then, I have outlined a way in which both intentional and unintentional self-deception can occur in a single agent, without resorting to homuncular subsystems. In the two preceding chapters, the notions of unconscious partitioning of beliefs and (hidden) intentions were employed, together with an outline of the mechanisms and processes by which self-deceptive belief formation is achieved. Crucially, self-deception is about the motivated disavowal of anxiety-heightening unfavourable beliefs and intentions. A failure to understand this point leads us either to postulate implausible models of the mind or reject as incoherent and impossible a literal understanding of this psychological phenomenon.

It is time to examine one doctrine that has often been considered to be a theory of self-deception. I refer to psychoanalysis and, in particular, to Freud's explanation of the irrational mind.

Chapter 7

The Freudian Explanation of Irrationality

'I did not know these things at that time, nor did I advert to them. They beat upon my eyes on every side, and yet I did not see them.'

Augustine, Confessions III 7

Freud's complex survey of the mind is based around the ideas of unconscious determination, desire and meaning. Psychoanalytic theory attributes to agents a whole series of motives of which they are unaware and, in some cases, cannot access without therapy. Freudian theory countenances the view that our first-person accounts of our actions are not always reliable and that hidden forces motivate many of our actions. While an agent interprets the motivation for his action in one way, an analyst can confer on it a different meaning or motivation based on information volunteered by the subject. This has given rise to a popular view that Freudian psychoanalysis is essentially a theory of human self-deception.

In this chapter, I want to explore whether the Freudian account of irrationality involves the kind of self-deception I outlined in the preceding chapters. I will argue that while there are certain points of similarity between the two

103

accounts, the Freudian cases are also radically different from 'ordinary' self-deception. For while failures of self-understanding and self-knowledge are implicit in Freudian theory, they do not revolve around specific paradoxes of belief, intention or will. In other words, the Freudian categorisation of irrational symptoms relies upon a non-standard mode of psychological explanation.

Why Freud seems to offer a theory of self-deception: The first hint of self-deception in Freudian theory is suggested by his theory of the divided mind. The clinical behaviours Freud studied seemed to manifest the conflict of the individual with himself, a clash between forces within the person. This suggested a theoretical mental structure in which there were different layers comprising the human mind, with consciousness merely the tip of the mental iceberg. The Cartesian equation of mentality with consciousness was exposed as an untenable hypothesis, a myth to be shattered for eternity.

In *An Autobiographical Study*, Freud made his famous denial of the equation of mentality with consciousness. Freud warned us that our conventional equation of mentality with consciousness 'disrupts psychical continuities, plunges us into the insoluble difficulties of psychophysical parallelism, is open to the reproach that for no obvious reason it over-estimates the part played by consciousness, and that it forces us prematurely to abandon the field of psychological research without being able to offer us any compensation from other fields'.[68]

Throughout his working life, Freud clearly believed that consciousness comprised only a small and transient part of mental life. Consciousness was the sum total of all that we were aware of, and underlying it was a vast realm of ideas, affects and emotional forces whose operations were not immediately apparent. The preconscious straddled the conscious and the unconscious and was the reservoir of all our easily accessible memories.

While Freud was not the first person to discern the influence of the unconscious, he was, as Strachey put it, the man who made the unconscious 'real to us'. He provided an insight into its dynamic workings and repeatedly gave an empirical basis for this belief. The empirical evidence he adduced for this idea came initially from hysterical manifestations and post-hypnotic suggestion. Freud describes the mind of the hysterical patient as being 'full of active yet unconscious ideas'. The actions of the post-hypnotic subject were described in the same way:

> The real stimulus to the action being the order of the physician, it is hard not to concede that the idea of the physician's order became active too. Yet this last idea did not reveal itself to consciousness, as did its outcome, the idea of the action; it remained unconscious, and so it was active and unconscious at the same time.[69]

An analogy is already suggested between the division of mind into dynamically opposing substrata and the notion of weak partitioning in the explanation of self-deceptive beliefs. In this model, we have postulated that the coexisting incompatible beliefs are separated by some form of mental distance, such that at the time the subject is self-deceived, the unfavoured belief is inaccessible and does not co-occur in his stream of consciousness with the favoured belief.

In his later topographical model of the mind, the tripartite division between unconscious, preconscious and conscious was superseded by that of the id, superego and ego. The id is the most primitive part of the psychical apparatus, containing everything inherited and laid down in the psychical constitution. The ego is a part of the id that has been modified by contact with the external world and

105

which is, in consequence, an organised part of the human personality. It is fundamentally involved with self-preservation and must adapt to external events through flight, adaptation or activity. It must also deal with the internal pressures of the id and the superego. It gains control over the instinctive demands of the id, either by allowing them immediate discharge and satisfaction, postponing that satisfaction or suppressing the instinctual demands altogether. The superego is the voice of internalised morality and constitutes a third force, which the ego must take into account in its daily operations.

Freud and the second mind: At this stage, it is worth asking whether the psychoanalytic picture is based on a second-mind model. We can then see whether Freudian explanation is committed to the kind of person-divisive explanation suggested by Pears.

An incomplete and fragmentary reading of Freud, however, may certainly suggest that he was committed to a strongly partitive view of the mind. One point Freud made was that the postulation of the unconscious within oneself was analogous to the postulation of mental states in other people. As Freud pointed out, 'One did not hesitate to ascribe mental processes to other people, although one had no immediate consciousness of them and could only infer them from their words and actions.'[70] In *The Unconscious*, he said that 'psychoanalysis demands nothing more than that we should apply this process of inference to ourselves ... all the acts and manifestations which I notice in myself and do not know how to link up with the rest of my mental life must be judged as if they belonged to someone else...' Again in section 1 of *The Unconscious* he admitted that such an inference 'leads logically to the assumption of another, second consciousness which is united in one's self-with the consciousness one knows...'[71]

106

Elsewhere in *The Unconscious* he wrote that 'we are obliged to say of some of these latent states that the only respect in which they differ from conscious ones is precisely in the absence of consciousness.'[72] There were famous pathological cases, in particular those of Dr Azam of Bordeaux, which Freud refers to as evidence for the conceptual possibility of multiple personality.

However, the notion of an 'unconscious consciousness' is a conceptual absurdity and, as Freud would have it, not one that is preferable or more intelligible to an unconscious mental state. For it could hardly be meaningful to talk of a consciousness of which its possessor was unaware.

Freud suggested another important reason for rejecting the idea of an unconscious consciousness. Analytic investigation showed that the unconscious was characterised by processes which were alien to those of the conscious rational mind. Freud elaborated as follows in *The Unconscious*:

> ...analytical investigation reveals some of these latent processes as having characteristics and peculiarities which seem alien to us, or even incredible, and which run directly counter to the attributes of consciousness with which we are familiar.[73]

According to Freud, processes in the unconscious simply obey different laws from those in the preconscious ego. These include their 'exemption from mutual contradiction, primary process, timelessness and replacement of external reality by psychical reality'.[74] 'What is proved', Freud says, 'is not the existence of a second consciousness in us, but the existence of psychical acts which lack consciousness.'[75]

Freudian theory is not therefore committed to the radical compartmentalisation of agency that we find in Pearsian theory. In this sense, the theory survives the special criticisms made at the end of chapter 3 and remains a candidate for an empirical theory of self-deception.

Thus far the theory of the divided mind and the dynamic clash of psychical forces suggest a theory of self-deception. So too does the 'language' of resistance and repression which is the true cornerstone of psychoanalysis.

Repression: Repression is one of a number of defence mechanisms that the ego makes use of in its conflicts with dangers, both internal and external. Its function is to protect the ego from dangers or threats to its survival. If these threats are internal, they emanate from the id or the superego; if external, from the external world. According to Freud, 'the essence of repression lies in turning something away and keeping it at a distance from the conscious mind'.[76] One of the key features of repression, according to Freud, is that the analysand cannot form a proper conception of an object and instead displays some form of flight or anxiety towards it.

There is an intimate connection between resistance and repression. Freud noted the following:

> ... when we undertake to restore a patient, to relieve him of the symptoms of his illness, he meets us with a violent and tenacious resistance ... one hardly comes across a single patient who does not make an attempt at reserving some region or other for himself so as to prevent the treatment from having access to it.[77]

The forces of resistance counter the analyst's attempt to uncover the cause of a pathogenic process. Freud says that it is the ego which is responsible for putting repression into effect:

108

Repression proceeds from the ego when the latter – it may be at the behest of the superego – refuses to associate itself with an instinctual cathexis (energy) which has been aroused in the id.[78]

Why would the ego find it necessary at all to repress anything?[79] In Freud's topographical model of the mind, impulses unrestricted by the demands of morality, society or the external world reside in the cauldron of the id, where they seek immediate discharge according to the dictates of the pleasure principle. The id, lacking access to reality and the demands of civilised society, operates blindly and without regulation. The ego's need for repression comes about precisely because the material it encounters in the id is incompatible with its own nature. It is the incompatibility between the ego instincts (or instincts of self-preservation as Freud calls them) and the sexual or libidinal impulses of the id that causes repression.

Neuroses are generally expressions of conflict between the ego and those of the sexual impulses that are seen by the ego to be incompatible with its integrity. As Freud puts it, 'the ego wishes at all costs to retain its adaptability in relation to the real external world.'[80] In the second of his 'Two Encyclopaedia Articles', Freud again talks about the incompatibility between the sexual and ego instincts. Symptoms, he writes, 'come about by sexual instinctual impulses being rejected (repressed) by the subject's personality (his ego) and then finding expression through circuitous paths through the unconscious'.[81]

There certainly seem to be some similarities between self-deception and psychoanalytic theory in these respects. In the Freudian case, the language of repression and resistance undoubtedly reminds us of some key features of ordinary self-deception. The notion of the ego 'warding itself off from danger' is akin to the self-deceiver using a motivated strategy to hide away a belief which will cause anxiety. Freud thinks of resistance as a force that is 'resolved to hold onto illness' and 'defend against recovery'. We have similarly seen a form of evasive resistance in the way the glutton must keep her genuine motive hidden if she is to remain self-deceived. She stubbornly prevents the possibility of 'recovering' to a state of epistemic rationality, which she could achieve only through the rejection of her anxiety-lowering irrational beliefs.

So far, then, we have established that the Freudian language used to describe a clash of instinctual forces suggests something like self-deception. Freud, however, does not postulate a second mind as in the Pearsian fantasy. If we move from the basics of metapsychological theory to an examination of some Freudian case studies, we will see more clearly whether Freudian explanations are akin to those of ordinary self-deception.

Irrationality in psychoanalysis: Psychoanalytic theory investigates irrationality largely through its examination of the neuroses.[82] Irrationality is manifest in the formation of symptoms, such as compulsive actions, groundless fears, exaggerated responses and ill-conceived projects. Manifest in the subject's behaviour are 'thoughts in which he is in fact not interested' and 'impulses in himself ... which appear very strange to him', in addition to, 'actions the performance of which give him no enjoyment, but which it is quite impossible for him to omit'.[83] These are clearly contrarational constituents of their sufferers' mental lives and put a severe strain on their own sense of self-understanding. We will examine two of Freud's case studies in order to illuminate the logic of psychoanalytic explanation.

The Ratman: The case of the Ratman is one of Freud's most celebrated case studies. He displayed some of the neurotic symptoms mentioned earlier: compulsive impulses (to cut his throat and undergo a harmful diet), obsessive thoughts regarding death and torture, groundless fears that things would happen to loved ones and a series of wholly unintelligible actions. These were highly aberrant and seemingly unintelligible mental phenomena, clearly putting a severe strain on the Ratman's sense of self-understanding. Nevertheless, these phenomena were not radically alien psychological occurrences. The Ratman clearly believed that, in some way, these obsessional structures formed part of his mental life. What he could not do is make the crucial intelligible links that would enhance his self-knowledge. He was not suffering from madness but a rather severe and unusual form of irrationality. There was some meaningful relation between these symptoms and the rest of his mental life but the Ratman was unable to make the connection without the interpretative skills of an analyst. When he visited Freud, it became clear that his symptoms belonged to a structure of motivated self-misrepresentation that was susceptible to psychoanalytic explanation.

Freud untangled these symptoms and showed that they were motivated by conflicting attitudes: hatred of his father, contradicted by a strongly felt idealising love for him, and a competing love for other women. Central to this case is the Ratman's 'great obsessive fear'. The Ratman narrated to Freud a story that he was told by his military superior, the Captain. The Captain related to the Ratman an account of a punishment that was used on prisoners in the east. The victim would be carefully tied down and a pot, containing rats, turned upside down on his buttocks. The rats would be left to gnaw their way out through the victim's anus. The retelling of this horrific story provoked a sense of shock and horror in the Ratman, which he believed was due to the horror and cruelty of the punishment. As he told it, however, the Ratman thought of the punishment being applied to his father. Initially, the Ratman was horrified at the thought that such appalling torture could be applied to his father. Freud then goes on to note that the Ratman displayed ambivalent feelings. For 'at all the more important moments while he was telling his story his face took on a very strange, composite expression'. The horror that the Ratman expressed was, in fact, a 'horror at pleasure of his own of which he was unaware'.[84] The idea of the rat torture being applied to his father was something that the Ratman unconsciously desired, based as it was on a still unconscious hate.

The Ratman had originally been reluctant to spell out the story to Freud. When asked to recount the story, the patient, 'broke off, got up off the sofa, and begged me to spare him the recital of the details'.[85] Recounting the story would have caused grave anxiety to the Ratman, and Freud interpreted this, too, as wish fulfilling. The patient not only gained pleasure at imagining this torture but wanted to be punished for it. When the Ratman told the story, he expressed a wish of what he would like to happen to his father, but this wish was then subsequently repudiated, causing him to desire to be punished. Now the Ratman cowed before Freud because, as a result of transference, Freud had been substituted for his father in the Ratman's imagination. In such a capacity, Freud was going to beat the Ratman for his sadistic wish.

At the root of the conflicted states was the Ratman's unconscious hatred for his father. Naturally, the Ratman denied that he hated his father as he felt a strong idealising love for him. For this reason the Ratman wondered 'how he could possibly have had such a wish, considering that he loved his father more than anyone else in the world'.[86] The main reason for the inaccessibility of the hatred was due to its being repressed. Repression rendered inaccessible the Ratman's strong hatred for his father. The next question is: just why had this been repressed?

Freud believed that the Ratman's symptoms had come about through a conflict between his sexual impulses and the imagined prohibitive demands of his father. What Freud did was to trace the aetiology of his symptoms to a set of motivated conflicts – centrally, to the fact that he hated his father, something which was opposed by his very strongly felt idealising love for him. Specifically, the Ratman's deep hostility to his father was related to the imagined hostility of the Ratman's father to his son's sexual impulses when he (Ratman) was a child.

The hostility was derived from the Ratman's memory of a traumatic beating by his father, received when he was an infant. This was something to which the young Ratman had responded with such vehement abuse that his shocked father had terminated the beating. The Ratman remembered that he had been beaten after wetting his parents' bed, after having lain in it. According to Freud's interpretation, however, the beating was administered because of the boy's masturbation. He hypothesised that it had put an effective end to the masturbation, but had led the Ratman to think of his father as frustrating his son's sexual pleasures:

> This punishment, according to my hypothesis, had, it was true, put an end to his masturbating, but ... it had left behind it an ineradicable grudge against his father and had established him for all time in his role of an interferer with the patient's sexual enjoyment.[87]

From the age of six, the Ratman remembered thinking that he wanted to see young girls naked, but was anxious that if he entertained such thoughts, his father might die. Also, at the age of twelve he remembered thinking that a girl he

113

especially liked would be kinder to him if his father died or if some catastrophe befell him.

Another principal conflict concerned the Ratman's 'lady'. His father had expressed discontent with his son's choice of partner, as she was a poor woman with few means. He had also encouraged him to marry a richer girl. The Ratman said that he remembered thinking, before his father had died, that his father's death could come to his advantage: he could receive some of his father's will and then be rich enough to marry the girl. He was worried, however, that his marriage could harm his father in the next world.

We can clearly detect the sense of continual opposition between the boy's desire for the gratification of his sexual (and later marital) impulses and the imagined prohibitive demands of his father. The only way to overcome this barrier to his satisfaction was to imagine his father as dead; hence the parricidal wish he harboured, and the symptoms envisaging terrible things happening to his father which expressed this wish. Naturally, such symptoms had brought upon them the force of repression.

The Tablecloth Lady: Another well-known case in the Freudian literature is that of the Tablecloth Lady. The lady met Freud once at her own house after developing a rather disturbing obsessional symptom. She would repeatedly run from her room into a neighbouring one, take up a particular position next to a table on which there was a stained tablecloth, and summon her maid. When the maid arrived, she would tell her to go on a particular pointless errand or simply dismiss her. Naturally, the Tablecloth Lady was puzzled at her own activity and sought therapy as a result.

The explanation of her bizarre activity emerged during analysis and came entirely at the prompting of the patient herself. The lady recounted the events of her wedding night, an episode from some years past. On her wedding night, her husband had repeatedly come into her room to perform the sexual act. Each time he came in, however, he found to his embarrassment that he was impotent. The next morning he came into her room and poured some red ink on her bedclothes in the place where a bloodstain would have been appropriate, so as to avoid embarrassment when the maid came in. He wanted the maid to think that lovemaking had taken place the night before as a means of affirming his sexual potency. However, he poured the ink in the wrong spot.

The meaning of the lady's present symptoms became clearer both to the lady and to Freud during analysis. The lady was basically identifying with her husband, and her actions in the symptoms all indicated an imitation of the events that took place that night. The summoning of the maid was designed to reflect the events that would have taken place the first morning after the wedding when the maid entered the nuptial room.

The lady explained that when she took up her position beside the table, there was a prominent stain on the tablecloth. She also stood by the table in such a way that the maid could not possibly fail to notice it. The table and cloth that she stood beside represented, according to Freud, the bed and bedsheet. When she ran from one room to another, she was imitating her husband running into the bedchamber on their wedding night. When she placed the stain on the tablecloth, she was imitating what had happened on that night when they wanted to pour ink on the bedsheet to avoid admitting that the husband was impotent. The placing of the ink on the tablecloth represented the staining of the bedclothes, but this time the Tablecloth Lady made sure it was done 'correctly'.

No doubt, the incorrectly placed stain would have caused shame to her and her husband, as it would have signified the absence of prior sexual contact the night before. Now that the stain was correctly placed in front of the maid, the lady was in effect saying that they need not have been ashamed, for he was not impotent. The symptom therefore had a corrective facility. Now that the stain had been correctly placed on the tablecloth (bedclothes), it was obvious that sexual activity had taken place and that the lady had nothing to be ashamed of. The woman ultimately was acting out an imaginary fantasy of the non-impotence of her husband.

Similarities between psychoanalytic explanation and self-deception: Having described two classic case studies, we are in a better position to draw comparisons and contrasts with ordinary self-deception. I will suggest that there are three important respects in which the case studies are like the typical everyday self-deception we examined in chapters 1–6.

Self-knowledge is hidden: In a purposive and motivated way, both the Ratman and the Tablecloth Lady had an important item of self-knowledge hidden from them. Let us take the case of the Ratman first.

At one level he believed that he loved and did not hate his father. This would have been apparent to him if he had summoned up images of his father in everyday life. Underlying this conscious affection lay a deep reservoir of unconscious hate, fear and resentment, but the 'truth' concerning these mental states was hidden from him. Until he went into therapy, he did not remember the beating administered by his father or the other episodes of sexual frustration that he had suffered. Nor could he have appreciated the parricidal wish residing in his unconscious. His symptoms, as we said earlier, did not spring from nowhere, but were clearly connected with the rest of

116

his mental life. The Ratman was unable independently to discover how this was so. If we were trying to establish the Ratman case as one of ordinary self-deception, we could plausibly construct the following type of schema:

i) Ratman believed that he loved his father and did not hate him.
ii) Ratman actually hated his father while also loving him.
iii) Ratman believed he loved his father because the recognition or belief that he hated his father was too painful to bear.
iv) Repression of proposition/judgement 'I hate my father' then took place because it was too painful a belief to acknowledge, while overall the Ratman did hate his father.
v) The suggestion that the Ratman's irrational and promoted symptoms were caused by his hatred of his father was met with resistance and denial because the belief that he hated him was too painful to recognise.

The resemblance between this explanatory schema and that provided for cases of ordinary self-deception is obvious. The Ratman, like familiar self-deceivers, lacked access to an important mental state, without which he was unable to attain true self-understanding. This element in his mental jigsaw puzzle seemed to forever elude his grasp.

The same analysis is true of the lady. After the events of the wedding night were repressed, the lady lacked a true sense of self-understanding. Before undergoing therapy, a vital part of her psychological life was a mere blank for her. She was denied access to a fundamental piece of self-knowledge, realisation of which would plausibly have caused her great pain and discomfort. It took expert therapy for her to gain a more accurate self-understanding, based on carefully guided introspective analysis.

Motivated burial: A state of 'motivated ignorance' is also central to both of these psychoanalytic case histories. The Ratman's symptoms, like the obsessive-compulsive symptoms displayed by the lady, were not accidental mental phenomena. The symptoms instead showed a decidedly purposeful character. The Ratman was warded away from a realisation of his parricidal wish because of his ego's need to protect its own integrity. The hostile and murderous impulse towards the Ratman's father constituted an internal anxiety-provoking threat that created the need for a repressive response. The end result was the burial of this impulse, which served a vital, ego-protecting function and spared the Ratman considerable anxiety. Similarly, the painful memories of the Tablecloth Lady's wedding night needed to be repressed in order to reduce her shame and low self-esteem.

We have seen the important ego-protective function served by favoured beliefs in ordinary self-deception. Promoted or favourable beliefs help reduce the unpleasantness of some painful or anxiety-provoking belief or strongly held suspicion. By doing this, self-esteem can be raised and anxiety or fear correspondingly reduced.

Causal influence of buried material: Neither in psychoanalytic case studies nor in cases of self-deception are buried mental states inert. In the psychoanalytic cases, we have assumed that a buried or repressed item is banished from conscious access but nonetheless lies deeply hidden in the id. It is here left to exert a considerable influence on the individual, constantly seeking and obtaining expression in symptomatic form. The Ratman disavows a hostile, parricidal impulse but then refuses to completely

118

abandon it. It is secretly held on to, where it festers in the unconscious and is causally efficacious in the production of his later symptoms. Similarly, we assume that an individual self-deceptively has an irrational belief only because of the presence of an anxiety-provoking and unfavourable belief. This latter unfavourable belief exerts some causal influence on the person's thinking and behaviour.

Psychoanalysis as different to core self-deception: Despite superficial similarities, the case studies are explained through different modes of psychological explanation to those of ordinary self-deception.

No doxastic paradox: In neither of our case studies does the paradox of belief have any meaningful application. Neither the Tablecloth Lady nor the Ratman suffer the motivated inconsistency of conflicting beliefs that characterises normal self-deceivers. There is no evidence that the lady has any inaccessible belief about why she is running around the table performing this strange ritual or that she believes deep down that her husband was impotent. By the same token, she appears to lack any favoured belief that her husband was potent. Similarly, it is gratuitous to assert that the Ratman secretly believes that his father frustrated his sexual wishes and that it would be better to see him tortured. The inaccessible beliefs that they do possess are not the ones required for us to maintain that they simultaneously hold inconsistent beliefs. The tactic of attributing contradictory beliefs in the psychoanalytic case studies is gratuitous and only seems necessary to defend psychoanalytic theory as a theory of ordinary self-deception.

At no point either is the concept of intention relevant to these cases. The lady did not rationally plan to form symptoms as a form of surrogate satisfaction for an innate desire. Her action cannot be represented as 'the spilling of ink and the summoning of the maid as a means of correcting a painful event in the past'. The lady does not consciously reason that standing at the table and summoning the maid is a good way to avenge her late husband's embarrassment or correct his impotence. She has no such belief and nor does she have any beliefs about the ability to change the past or that tablecloths and bedclothes resemble each other. The judgement that 'I am running to the table and summoning the maid' exists in limbo, as she lacks grounds for assessing why she acts as she does. The judgement about what she is doing does not stand connected to other propositions in the normal way that beliefs relate holistically and logically to other propositional attitudes.

The neurotic symptoms in each case are the deep expressions of wishes that are subject to the rules governing wish fulfilment. In the case of the Tablecloth Lady, Freud said that the obsessional action 'represented her wish, in the manner of a dream, as fulfilled in a present-day action'.[88] The lady had an unconscious wish to correct her sense of shame at her husband's impotence; this was achieved by presenting the stain in the right place as if to say, 'My husband was not impotent after all; he had nothing to be ashamed about.' So the Tablecloth Lady's rituals are wish fulfilments, imaginative representations of a desired reality.[89]

Limited access to motive: Another crucial factor differentiating psychoanalytic case studies from cases of ordinary self-deception is the subject's access to their motives. Psychoanalytic cases involve unconscious motives that are radically inaccessible to their owners. These motives are unavailable to the subject through ordinary introspection and require specific therapy to uncover. There are certainly no visible signs that the Ratman or the lady realise deep down what motivates their bizarre activity.

They can be said to be deeply disconnected from their real psychological motive, lacking the necessary temporary glimpse of repressed impulses and ideas to break the cycle of their irrationality. What follows is that the concept of counter-evidence does not apply to psychoanalytic cases as it does to those of self-deception. There was probably never a time, prior to analysis, when the Ratman would have been able to seize on a piece of evidence that would have confirmed his true feelings for his father. The level of mental distance between inaccessible motives and conscious awareness would have been far wider than in cases of ordinary self-deception.

In cases of self-deception, subjects are not deeply disconnected from their motives. A probing and careful reflective analysis may be enough in cases of self-deception to cease believing irrationally. The deluded lover may come to think repeatedly that she is worse off staying with an untrustworthy lover than seeking romantic involvement elsewhere. In moments of clarity, she may well realise the true motives in her rationalisations and evasions of evidence.

There is a further interesting consequence to note. We have emphasised that in cases of self-deception, the promotion of irrational beliefs is a continual process that constantly engages the individual concerned. It is because a subject encounters both recurrent glimpses of a rational belief and challenges to a promoted belief, that the techniques of self-deception must continually be used. The motivated misrepresentation in self-deception is not a one-shot affair. In the analytic session, things are otherwise. In the case of the Ratman, we have seen that when an impulse is subject to repression, there is no need for this act of burial to be continually repeated, though resistance to the repressed impulses can be a continual process.

Responsibility: In the case studies we have looked at, the two individuals who displayed irrational symptoms were not responsible for their problems. I take it that in all cases of self-deception, the subjects in question fail to provide themselves with relevant epistemically rational beliefs. That is, they do not gather beliefs, or act in ways to gather beliefs, by using methods that will help secure them truthful representations of the world. Their resulting beliefs are not well grounded on the reasons they have for those beliefs. A failure to ensure that one has done all that is possible to gather true beliefs leads to what Hilary Kornblith has called 'epistemic irresponsibility'. Even in cases of tropistic biasing of data relevant to our beliefs, we can still become momentarily aware of what we ought rationally to believe despite the effects of the biasing that take place. A failure to notice the effects of such skews or biases would be sufficient to render a self-deceiver 'epistemically irresponsible'.

Given the deep inaccessibility of motives and the lack of counter-evidence postulated in psychoanalytic theory, it follows that the Ratman and the lady cannot resist the onset of their irrational symptoms. At no point are they able to gain any insight into why they display their bizarre impulses and symptoms. Instead, they are simply puzzled at their obsessive actions, thoughts and impulses. Their bizarre and inconsistent behaviours are generated by a variety of psychic processes which take place at a purely unconscious level. Without insight and the ability to use introspection to change behaviour, the Ratman and the Tablecloth Lady cannot be said to share the moral responsibility of ordinary self-deceivers.

The Freudian strategy paradox

Freud, Sartre and the censor: In our discussion of the Ratman, we looked at the role of repression and resistance in creating a type of self-deceptive activity. We noted the reasons for material becoming repressed and the mechanisms by which this took place. We concentrated less on the dynamics of repression and the problems this created for Freud's account. It now emerges that a version of the strategy paradox might apply to psychoanalytic theory. Sartre certainly believed that Freud's enterprise, particularly with its emphasis on repression and resistance, was open to criticism.

The focus of Sartre's argument is on the Freudian notion of the censor. According to Sartre, resistance is 'objective behaviour, apprehended from without', according to which, 'the patient shows defiance, refuses to speak, gives fantastic accounts of his dreams'. Hence, 'it is a fair question to ask what part of himself can thus resist'.[90] What Sartre means to discover is what part of the analysand attempts to evade the analyst when a systematic attempt is made to coax the nature of repressed impulses.

The impulse is not simply hidden from other people, such as one's analyst, for defence is characterised by Freud as a hiding of 'something from oneself'. It is not conceived as an act of deception. The ego cannot hide an impulse from the id, for the impulse to be hidden comes directly from the id, so the id's deception would be impossible. The impulse is not hidden either from the superego, for it is often the superego that perceives the id impulse and then induces the anxiety that leads to ego repression. By the same token, it appears to make no sense to talk of the impulse being hidden from the ego, for it is the ego that executes the defensive manoeuvre and represses material.

According to Sartre it is only the censor mechanism that is able to do this. The censor, according to Sartre, 'alone can comprehend the questions or revelations of the psychoanalyst as approaching more or less near to the real drives which it strives to repress ... it alone knows what it is repressing'. Now, the problem of repression in general is that it involves both locating a thing to be concealed and repressing and disguising it. The question to ask is, 'how could the censor discern the impulses needing to be repressed without being conscious of discerning them'.[91] We can immediately recognise echoes of the strategy paradox here. This paradox was concerned with how we could intentionally hide something from ourselves when the very act of hiding would give the game away; knowledge would subvert the effort to conceal knowledge. For Sartre, the censor is in bad faith. It would seem as if the censor would have to be conscious of the drive to be repressed in order not to become conscious of it. The separation of consciousness from the censor does not help to resolve the problem, for the censor must be aware of its activities in order to be able to recognise the repressed material and censor it. According to Sartre:

> ... the very essence of the reflexive idea of hiding something from oneself implies the unity of one and the same psychic mechanism and consequently a double activity in the heart of unity, tending on the one hand to maintain and locate the thing to be concealed and on the other to repress and disguise it ... each of the aspects of this activity is complementary to the other; that is, it implies the other in its being ... psychoanalysis has merely localised this double activity of repulsion and attraction on the level of the censor...[92]

One point to make is that the censor mechanism had only a relatively brief history in Freudian theory. The censorship of dreams is importantly mentioned in *The Interpretation of Dreams* and in the first set of *Introductory Lectures*, but the idea was later superseded by the concept of the ego in his topographical theory of the mind.

In 1937 Freud resolved to grapple anew with this 'problem'. In his paper 'The Splitting of the Ego in the Process of Defence', Freud saw a new way of generalising the role of the ego in defence. The traditional split in the topographical theory of mind was between the ego, the id and the superego. According to the 1937 theory, the result of defence is to create a split within the ego itself. A complex of motive, purpose, feeling and drives is split off from the more rational system of the ego. The complex may be constituted by ego-alien erotic impulses or by competitive or dangerous impulses to harm another. This nucleus is split off from the ego because it fails to reflect the richness of the ego's learning or identifications. Essentially, it lacks the maturity and adaptability of the rest of the ego. Once this nucleus does form, the ego regards it as an alien force which exists outside of itself. It has an essentially 'not me' quality. For Freud, this defensive process is not something that *happens* to the ego but something that the ego *does* – a motivated strategy. The warding off we get in repression and resistance is something undertaken not by the id, superego or censor but by a part of the ego itself.

Freud's descriptions of this process of ego-splitting are similar to the process of disavowal in self-deception. The ego's defensive processes are analogous to the way that the person wards off unwanted beliefs and evidence while self-deceived. The unwanted mental states also have an alien quality which, as I said, is largely expressed by an inability to avow them. In his 1937 paper, Freud describes repressive defence in terms such as 'disavowal' and 'rejection'. He also talks of the aim of defence as being to 'spit out' something. In *An Outline of Psychoanalysis*, Freud addresses again the issue of the splitting of the ego in the context of neurosis. He writes as follows:

...the ego often enough finds itself in the position of fending off some demand from the external world which it finds distressing and that this is effected by means of a disavowal of the perceptions which bring to knowledge this demand from reality. Disavowals of this kind occur very often ... and whenever we are in a position to study them they turn out to be half measures, incomplete attempts at detachment from reality. The disavowal is always supplemented by an acknowledgement; two contrary and independent attitudes always arise and result in the situation of there being a spitting of the ego.[93]

Classic self-deceptive behaviour involves the active disavowal and repudiation of a rational but anxiety-provoking belief. The metaphor of 'spitting out' is a useful one to employ in describing the manner of the self-deceptive agent's disavowal, denial and evasion of an unfavoured belief. If we remove the clinical context in describing the aetiology of neurotic disorders, Freud could easily be describing the contradictory belief states we get in self-deception.

How well does Freud meet the strategy paradox? In one sense Sartrean paradox remains, for we can ask how a part of the ego keeps itself unconscious of splitting itself off from the alien part of itself. It has to protect itself from the id derivative, from that alien impulse which is incompatible with itself. If it is unconscious, is this dynamically motivated? If so, we would need to presume that there is a second-order defensive manoeuvre which is consciously motivated and which is responsible for the unconsciousness of the ego, while at the same time repressing the id material. Is there then a third-order defensive manoeuvre, conscious of a part of the ego, which renders the second-order manoeuvre unconscious? If so, this simply reduplicates the 'infinite regress' problem we encountered in the solution to the strategy paradox.

Freud himself seems to offer no answer to this question, at least not in the paper he wrote in 1937. This paper was unfinished and represented a very late revision to his theory. We can at least be sure that Freud was aware of a new and important facet to psychoanalytic theory, and this involved something like a hint of the dynamic puzzle of self-deception.

Freudian freedom: Freud offered a way of curing or eliminating an irrational but motivated failure of self-knowledge. Psychoanalytic therapy was partly conceived as a liberation of the analysand (patient undergoing analysis) from internal instinctual forces. Freud's aim was to undo the patient's resistance, to bring repressed material back into the analysand's consciousness and to release pent-up energies that had become repressed in earlier life. Sufferers like the Ratman and the Tablecloth Lady suffered from the compulsive repetition of the past or, as Freud would have it, 'the return of the repressed'. By making their hidden and repressed energies come back into conscious view, they were given a new perspective on life.

Through therapy, they were granted greater freedom as agents. This happened on two levels. Firstly, patients were relieved of their troublesome neuroses, which had caused them stress, anxiety and even fear. Secondly, they also gained a greater autonomy through being aware of their internal motives, projects, fears or anxieties. Psychoanalytic therapy brought about a state of heightened self-knowledge and self-awareness, principally through uncovering what once lay deep in the realms of the unconscious and subjecting it to conscious scrutiny.

So the Freudian message now is about giving people freedom to pursue their projects without hindrance from the forces of the past. Freud summarises the idea in his famous maxim: 'Where id was, ego shall be.' Once the individual is freed from the bonds of irrationality, greater self-knowledge can be acquired.

To conclude, it only appears that Freud offers a theory of self-deception. His patients in the classic case studies were deprived of a vital piece of self-knowledge, which prevented them from leading free and symptom-less lives. While these failures of self-knowledge were not accidental but sprang from basic motives, the psychological explanations of their irrationality did not involve the normal categories of mentalistic explanation. It would therefore be a mistake to believe that Freud was offering a theory of self-deception as we commonly understand it.

Chapter 8

The Irrationality of Self-deception

'The wise man proportions his belief to the evidence.'

David Hume

How irrational are self-deceivers? This entirely depends on the type of irrationality and, by implication, the type of *rationality* we are talking about. Traditionally, there are two ways to conceive of rationality. The first concerns the rationality of our beliefs and is usually called epistemic rationality. The second concerns the rationality of our actions and is called pragmatic rationality.

In ascribing rationality to people, two elements stand out – consistency and goal-directedness. Rational beliefs or actions are those things that, *ceteris paribus*, we ought to adopt given our fundamental goals. In other words, we are required to act and think in ways that accord with the goals that we possess. What are these goals? For cognitive or descriptive beliefs, that class of beliefs which seeks to understand and explain the workings of the world, this could simply be described as 'truth'. We ought to believe those things about the world that are true or as close to the truth as possible, given our level of intelligence and capacity for acquiring accurate data about the environment. This is a key requirement, for what constitutes a rational cognitive belief will vary from one person to another and from one time period to another.

Ascriptions of irrationality are almost entirely agent-specific. It may be perfectly reasonable, if misguided, for a five-year-old to believe in Santa Claus, but completely irrational for his elder brother. The five-year-old is unable to see the Santa Claus story as a part of a pervasive and powerful part of contemporary cultural mythology. As he cannot detect the elaborate deception practised on him, we would not say his belief was irrational. Given access to different information and the ability to reasonably judge what he is told, his elder brother is in a different position. If he believes in Santa Claus, he will find it harder for his belief to be deemed rational. This is crucial, because all self-deception operates against a background of avoidable irrationality, where greater diligence and objectivity would allow people to think and behave in more reasonable ways.

On the one hand, ascriptions of rationality operate in a thoroughly relativistic way, depending entirely on the individual's set of belief states, his access to information and the level of his intelligence. We should always talk of whether a *person's* belief is rational, given the factors we have mentioned. On the other hand, the *rules* for ascribing rationality appear to be fixed and absolute, applying equally to all agents.

Pragmatic rationality is an altogether different type of irrationality. Unlike epistemic rationality, it is not of necessity dictated by considerations of truth and intellectual probity, though there is a close connection between the two. An agent is pragmatically rational when he acts in ways that he thinks will help to secure him the things that he wants. To use the technical jargon of game theory, a pragmatically rational agent will seek to do those things that he thinks will maximise his 'expected utility'.

I contend that in all cases of self-deception, a self-deceived agent holds beliefs that are necessarily epistemically irrational. That is to say that the agent's self-deceptive beliefs, which are neither necessary truths nor perceptual or experiential beliefs, are not epistemically rational, and this is sufficient for them to be deemed epistemically irrational. However, there is room for debate about whether self-deceivers are also irrational by the standards of pragmatic rationality.

Epistemic irrationality: If an agent's beliefs are to be epistemically irrational, then they must satisfy at least one of a number of important conditions:

Firstly, an agent's belief that p will be epistemically irrational if the belief is not well founded on the reasons a and b that are used to support it. That is to say that if reasons a and b do not provide any logical or argumentative support for the belief in question, then the agent's belief cannot be epistemically rational. From the mere fact that the glutton desires to believe that she is a modest eater, it does not follow that she is a modest eater. Hence she lacks a sound reason to believe that she is a modest eater. This is because there is no logical connection between a desire for x to be true and x being true.

Secondly, an agent's belief that p will be epistemically irrational when the belief has not been acquired through a reliable procedure or method. It is notoriously difficult to specify general conditions for reliability, as these will vary with the beliefs one adopts. If one wishes to find out what the weather will be like the following week, it will not do to ask the village idiot or decide the matter on the toss of a coin. This is an unreliable way of gathering evidence on which a subsequent belief will be based. Though one may subsequently acquire a correct belief, this is more a matter of luck than intellectual appropriateness. In general, reasons and reliability come together. For as Nozick suggests, if we ground our beliefs on a sound reason-based approach, we are thereby adopting a reliable means of acquiring good beliefs.

Thirdly, an agent's belief that p is epistemically irrational if, despite the supporting reasons a and b providing argumentative support for a belief, the supporting reasons are not themselves justified. In general for empirical beliefs, this means that we need proper evidence for our beliefs and we should withhold assent to any belief if this has not been provided. It may be prima facie rational for Carlos to believe that he will pass his test if his instructor indicates this to him. In the desire to allay anxiety about an impending fail, however, Carlos radically misinterprets his instructor's remarks, thus leading to a false and irrational belief in his driving abilities. While the instructor's positive remarks would have provided grounds for believing rationally that he would pass, there were also grounds to question the interpretation of the remarks in the first place.

Finally, an agent's belief that p will be epistemically irrational if, despite that belief being well founded on reasons a and b and despite a and b themselves being justified, there are alternative and better grounds a1 and b1 for an alternative belief q that the agent ought to acknowledge. The agent, because of a self-deceptive bias, will ignore a1 and b1 and thus fail to acquire the more reasonable belief q. Carlos thinks he is justified in believing he will pass the test because he was successful in carrying out a simple three-point turn during his previous lesson. The successful completion of a three-point turn, itself a difficult manoeuvre, seems to provide rational grounds for confidence when the test approaches. His confidence is ill placed, though. For he forgets that during the same lesson, he nearly crashed his car on several occasions and failed

132

to carry out some crucial operations. His anxious desire to believe he will pass the test, however, causes him to skew his recall of his past performance, thus leaving him with an epistemically irrational belief.

There are many different levels of epistemic irrationality taking place in the examples we have used so far. The glutton fails to provide herself with a sound argumentative basis for the belief in her modest eating habits. Her reason for this belief is essentially a desire to believe she is not a glutton, but the content of that reason does not provide a logical link to the content of her belief. Furthermore, in order to obtain evidence for her belief, she consults selective and biased sources and does not adopt the neutral, detached perspective on her condition that she would apply to other people. She therefore fails the second epistemic rationality test. Thirdly, even when she discovers grounds for her belief – say, one of her diary entries – these are dubious. She forgets that the entries were written at a time when she was sensitive to the gluttony problem and therefore deliberately minimised all mention of highly fattening foods. Fourthly, even when a diary entry reliably confirms what she wants to see, she ignores the totality of evidence that would provide her with grounds for a less favoured belief. She fails epistemic rationality criteria on all four counts.

I have stressed all along that the irrationality of the self-deceiver is due to a failure to apply his or her own standards of rationality. This is equivalent to saying that one cannot cheat at a game unless one knows its rules and knows what it is like to play by the rules. Being honest about oneself and one's commitments and evaluating sensitive personal issues with a desire for truth and accuracy is the norm of epistemic rationality. It is only when one is sensitive to these norms but fails to abide by them that one can then be irrational. In these cases, irrationality is fundamentally played out against an appreciation of rationality.

Given this fact, one may well ask how we can hold people guilty of being irrational when they are subject to the automatic cognitive skews we outlined in chapter 4. One might argue that all that is happening in these cases is that someone who desires to believe something about themselves comes under the accidental and unintended influence of 'cold' forces working from beneath a conscious level. As they are at the mercy of mental forces of which they are unaware and which they do not intend to trigger, they cannot be deemed irrational in the normal sense. This is a view that Donald Davidson appears to accept. According to Davidson:

> ... irrationality appears only when rationality is evidently appropriate: where both cause and effect have contents that have the sort of logical relations that make for reason and its failure. Events conceived solely in terms of their physical or physiological properties cannot be judged as reasons ... if we think of the cause (of self-deception) in a neutral mode, disregarding its mental status as a belief or other attitude ... merely as a force that works on the mind – then we fail to explain irrationality... Blind forces are in the category of the non-rational, not the irrational.[94]

I agree with Davidson that if we simply invoke cold forces as causal agents of self-deception, then we are looking at the realm of the non-rational rather than the irrational. However, I have been at pains to stress the essential role of beliefs and desires in this process. In self-deception, the biasing desire is the essential causal trigger which sets off

134

these mechanisms. In addition, in a true case of self-deception the unfavoured rational belief is held deep down by the individual. It is a lurking suspicion capable of generating psychic conflicts and anxious repudiation. Even though the glutton has misrepresented her activities to herself due to cognitive subpersonal machinery, she remains conflicted because the opposite belief is held at a deeper level.

We can speculate that when this unfavoured belief rears its ugly and unwanted head, the mechanisms continue to operate to remind her of the favoured belief. Thus, the memories supporting the favoured belief (the diary entries) will become vivid again. Her desire to believe she is not a glutton will allow these data-distortion mechanisms to continue operating. Furthermore, the person certainly ought to see that their resulting favourable belief is the end product of a series of data-distortion mechanisms and motivationally based skews.

Pragmatic irrationality: We said that pragmatic rationality has as its goal the maximisation of efficiency in achieving those things the agent wants. I contend that there is a close connection between epistemic and pragmatic rationality. This is normally because in order to achieve what we want in the world, we usually need to have a truthful or accurate representation of what the world is like. If I want to survive, I must consistently avoid eating poisonous foods. But in order to do this, I need to know which foods are poisonous and which are good for my health. This information will more likely be gained through a reliable belief-forming process. Consulting an article written by an expert will prove more rewarding than simple trial and error.

In some situations, however, things are not quite the same. One may be pragmatically rational through having

135

an epistemically irrational belief. We can see this in the case of Ike, the skilful prankster. He sets out to produce within himself an epistemically irrational belief that he performed well in class, but it is also one that serves his purposes. The belief has the effect of boosting his performance and bringing greater rewards in his future academic endeavours. So the inculcation of an epistemically irrational belief can bring him rewards and potentially maximise his expected utility.

However, I contend that in none of the cases that we have looked at can we be *certain* that the agents are acting in pragmatically rational ways. One bad reason for thinking that all self-deception must be in one's psychological self-interest is the argument that self-deception is a highly adaptive form of behaviour. I will briefly spell out this argument.

Evolutionary theory tends to accept that humans do not behave altruistically in the ancestral environment unless there is a genetic benefit accruing from this. In informational terms, this means that humans do not necessarily provide accurate information to other people if this confers a benefit to the recipient and a disadvantage to the sender of information. In the context of self-relevant information, it might therefore become adaptive to distort the truth and deceive other people if this confers advantages. A male might deceive a female by exaggerating his sexual prowess or hiding his lack of monogamy in order to mate with her and thereby pass his genes on to the next generation.

Evolution favours the capacity to deceive others and also seems to favour the detection of this deception. Deceit, in other words, helps bring about the selection of deception-detectors. This in turn arguably creates the need to improve deception strategies by better concealing the telltale signs that deception is taking place. One way to do this is to believe one's own lies. According to Trivers, this creates the need for a primitive form of self-deception by 'rendering some facts and motives unconscious so as not to betray – by the subtle signs of self-knowledge – the deception being practised'.[95] If we believe our own lies it makes us harder to get caught, because there is no conscious awareness of deceit.

It is not my intention here to get bogged down in the long-running debate about the validity of sociobiological theories. My interest is in the relevance of this argument to questions about the pragmatic rationality of self-deception. Let us suppose that the preceding analysis is correct and self-deception developed to make our lies more believable. We could speculate that it helped us secure for ourselves greater sexual satisfaction as hunter-gatherers, relative to our competitors, in the ancestral environment. Specifically, it meant that we were able to have sex with mates (and thereby pass on our genes to the next generation) who would otherwise have disregarded us as liars. This is no argument, however, for the pragmatic rationality of self-deception now.

If self-deception in the ancestral environment became an adaptive facility, it did so not through a process of conscious reasoning or reflective choice by primitive humans, but simply because mutant genes subtly altered the ways we thought and behaved. For the lucky few, the genetic alterations would have involved the development of behavioural mechanisms in which the telltale signs of deception became gradually hidden. Through the logic of natural selection, this would have ensured that self-deceptive-behaviour genes were passed on into the gene pool more readily than the genes correlated with the behaviour of bad liars. No choice was made in the ancestral environment that it would actually be better to hide deception, and there was no plausible intention to change behaviour patterns in order to do this. One reason is simply that this level of strategic intentional reasoning would have been impossible without a fully developed symbolic language replete with psychological attitudes of belief, intention and will. In a non-linguistic primitive society, such explicit propositional-attitude psychology would have been a near impossibility.

These considerations are important in assessing pragmatic rationality. Put simply, if an agent cannot assess the worth of engaging in a pursuit, activity or action, we cannot label him pragmatically rational or irrational. Irrationality is a failure of rationality and in the ancestral environment, without the elaborate apparatus of thought, language and higher level mental states, 'rationality' attributions would make no sense. So evolutionary theory cannot provide reasonable grounds for thinking that it is pragmatically rational to engage in self-deception in a contemporary environment.

Proponents of the evolutionary argument are also guilty of committing the genetic fallacy. The fallacy is of the form 'if x is descended from y, x must share some of the features of y.' The mere fact, though, that a genetic link exists between x and y is no reason to assume a commonality of features between x and y. It may be true that modern-day self-deception evolved from a highly primitive means of hiding deception. This is no argument for the view that the ancestral and modern behaviours are the same. What we are familiar with now is a more complex and varied psychological phenomenon.

In some situations, agents do benefit from deceiving themselves about their limitations. Sportsmen try to instil self-confidence after a good performance in the hope that it may breed better performance. For many sportsmen, the belief that they can win is a crucial part of emerging as winners. Take Miss America 1986, for example. Here we see the effects of positive thinking, which is a species of motivated belief. Kelly wanted p (to win the contest) and thought she had to believe p in order to get p. Therefore she made herself believe p as a means of achieving this when she did not believe she would get p in its absence. She allayed her doubts about p, doubts she would have entertained based on a rational weighting of evidence, and ended up (in her mind) reaping the rewards. Naturally, only if Kelly still harbours certain suspicions of poor performance, which she suppresses, can she be self-deceived. Nonetheless, it is not hard to appreciate the positive benefits accruing from this kind of psychological bootstrapping.

In other situations, certainly those most common to traditional self-deceptive behaviour, irrational suppression of doubt and suspicion is harmful. Here we must take into account both one's short- and long-term interests. Judged on their short-term interests, all the agents appear to do things that allay anxiety-provoking beliefs. Thus Carlos knows that he is more likely to allay anxiety by getting himself to believe that he will pass the driving test. If his goal is to alleviate anxiety and he knows that this can be achieved through believing he will pass the test, it becomes pragmatically rational to become self-deceived. The lady wants to avoid the pain that confronting her lover's activities will bring. The glutton fears the effects on her self-esteem of believing she has gluttonous habits. However, what Carlos surely wants is not simply to avoid a temporary anxiety about test failure but to be able to drive safely. The deluded lover wants a stable marriage or relationship. Neither does the glutton relish the prospect of heart disease or the other conditions that her gluttonous habits are storing up for her.

All these agents, while in the grip of their self-deception, are providing short-term satisfaction for themselves. What they are not considering is the consequent damage that may occur when they are released from the grip of irrational thinking. When they cease to be self-deceived, they may judge that short-term satisfaction, no matter what the probable later psychological cost, was a preferable state of affairs. Alternatively, they may judge that confronting their problems directly would be a surer route to attaining what they ultimately desire.

Imagine that at a later stage the deluded lover comes to see clearly the real nature of her relationship. Perhaps she finds her partner in bed with his lover, evidence that simply cannot be given a benign interpretation. The unavoidable break-up of the relationship causes her enormous pain and makes it far harder for her to trust future partners. It dawns on her that had she seen the light at an earlier stage and quickly ended the relationship, the later psychological costs would have been far smaller. A more pragmatically rational approach would have been to cause herself short-term pain to prevent greater long-term hardship.

To conclude, all self-deceivers necessarily have epistemically irrational beliefs. They need not, though they often do, act in ways that are pragmatically irrational.

Conclusion

Self-deception occurs because disturbing aspects of reality conflict with our cherished ideas, values and commitments. It is a motivated disavowal of unwelcome beliefs and nagging suspicions, which is often informed by a strong degree of intent and awareness. It behaves like a psychological narcotic that suppresses mental discomfort and anxiety. For all of us, there are worries and anxieties we would rather not confront and skeletons we would like to remain hidden. Self-deception is a way of trying to achieve both goals.

We can deceive ourselves about many things. Our health, sexual prowess, intellectual capacity and romantic involvements can all be of prime concern to us. The glutton who thinks she has a normal and healthy lifestyle, the deluded lover who fails to spot her partner's deception, the cancer patient who is oblivious to a health problem and the poor student who allays the fear of failure are all cases in which the balm of self deception is welcome. Of course, we could choose other examples but the classic signs of deeply irrational behaviour are unmistakeable.

Ultimately, self-deception always revolves around a question of self-esteem. To have strong self-esteem, one must believe that one's actions and commitments have intrinsic value and worth. This in turn both reflects and generates positive self-perceptions. We all want to believe

141

that we are worthwhile people, that we are competent, intelligent, honest and virtuous. Not only do we want to be people with those characteristics but also we need to appear that way. Success in life is largely about impression management, about pretending to others that we are so much better than we suspect ourselves to be. For it is an uncomfortable fact that there will always be a gap between our aspirations and reality. When we view ourselves in an idealising mirror we rarely see how we actually are. We have a self-image that relates to the kind of person we think we are and an ideal self which relates to how we would like to be. If there is a vast chasm between these two, then often low self-esteem results. If we cannot change reality, yet we refuse to be mediocre, it is our self-perceptions that must alter.

For O'Neill, life inescapably involved self-deception. If we strip people of all their illusions, they will view their lives as pitiful exercises in mediocrity. Self-deception allows us to believe that our lives transcend the ordinary. It is a psychological antidote to the frustration of reality when we are less than the sum of our aspirations.

Ultimately, there must be limits to the desirability of self-knowledge. Each individual cares more about himself than about any other person. We take great care to remember all our strengths (and parade them to others) and take pains to prevent the exposure of our flaws. As De Rochfecauld tells us, the huge flaws in other people matter less to us than the smallest flaw in ourselves. If we delve too closely into our natures, we might discover more of these flaws than we want to. The truth about ourselves is sometimes painful and when our cherished illusions are shattered, it may be difficult to recover. It is wrong to think that every gap in our self-knowledge requires the correction of insight, curative therapy or introspective analysis. Sometimes, ignorance can truly be bliss.

Before we conclude though that all self-deception is a harmless by-product of life's frustration, we must not forget its more sinister side. We saw at the outset that wilful inattention to danger among military leaders and commanders produced catastrophic results in the last war. Millions of lives were lost because of motivated errors of judgement and because the narcotic of denial was more attractive than confronting the truth. This puts the dangers of self-deception in a historical context but we see the same dangers in ordinary life.

Every day millions of people engage in an orgy of self-destructive behaviour. Smoking is both a dangerous and expensive habit, despite the best attempts by health experts to highlight its risks. Millions of adolescents experiment each year with dangerous intoxicating drugs. High profile cases of drug related deaths appear to make little impact here. Recent reports reveal a proliferation in the cases of sexually transmitted diseases among young sexually active adults. These and other cases show that our capacity for doing serious and long-term harm to ourselves remains undiminished.

We live in a society that craves short-term gratification. In our technological age, microwaves, fax machines, Internet connections and fast foods provide us with instant pleasure. In craving short-term gratification, our thinking bypasses the longer-term costs of our actions. If we are to prevent the dependency on all types of harmful substances, our culture must de-emphasize the benefits of short-term thinking. In a society that took to heart all the information about the risks to our health, we might see a small shift in lifestyle habits. We would have fewer illusions about avoiding premature death but a reduced tolerance for high-risk activities.

The main focus in this book has been on self-deception in a single person. There has been less stress on 'group self deception'. But the herd nonetheless has a capacity to erect a collective shutter in the face of reality's terrors. In other words, a group of people can collectively deceive themselves to produce a form of social myopia.

According to Walter Laqueur in *The Terrible Secret*, the reaction of Dutch and Hungarian Jewry to confirmation of the Final Solution could be likened to 'people facing a flood and who in contradiction of all experience believe that they will not be affected but are individually or as a group invulnerable'.[96] A far higher proportion of Dutch Jews were exterminated than was the case for every other Western European country. Elsewhere, he says that Polish Jews ought to have correctly understood Nazi designs after the deportations of Warsaw's Jews in July 1942. A Warsaw resident observing these events 'should have drawn the correct conclusions', however, 'the time and place were hardly conducive to detached, objective analysis'.[97] That many continued to harbour false hope merely showed that 'psychological pressures militated against rational analysis and created an atmosphere in which wishful thinking seemed to offer the only antidote to utter despair'.[98] For many of Eastern Europe's Jews, the message coming through about Nazism's genocidal intentions, 'left no room for hope and was therefore unacceptable'.[99]

Clearly, there is no acceptable monocausal explanation for the behaviour of all of Europe's Jewish communities during this tragic period. Information about the Final Solution varied from one community to the next. Soviet Jews, for example, were simply uninformed about what the Nazis were planning to do. By contrast, Danish Jews in 1943 came to hear that the Gestapo was planning to round them all up and the majority were able to escape to Sweden.[100] In other areas in Europe, rumours were circulated in varying fashions and, in some cases, details about extermination policy only leaked out slowly. Information

144

was not always clear and unambiguous. Unfortunately, the leaders of the different national communities were no wiser in this regard. Past history had shown the limited nature of pogroms and the hopes of many rested in a quick Allied victory. But it is conceivable that when some members of these communities 'discovered' the inevitable truth of the Final Solution, and their impending fate, the truth was too painful to bear. Many would have feared the full implications of confronting this 'evidence'. It was easier to ignore or wilfully misinterpret negative information and, by so doing, bring their impending fate closer. Instead of accepting the worst, comfort was sought in hope, optimism and denial.

Group self-deception can occur in more democratic contexts. Nowhere is this truer than in the context of national identity. All national identities are constructed on a carefully concocted bed of myths. The greatest myth is that of the permanence of nations and national traditions. In reality, nations as politically driven entities are relatively recent phenomena, which emerged in the aftermath of the French Revolution.

Often the myths and legends that underpin national identity revolve around more recent episodes in popular memory. Particularly in total war, issues of national identity come into very sharp focus. During the Second World War, each of the allied nations constructed a specific account of how the war was fought which involved a heavy dose of mythologizing. In each case, a popular account was created that highlighted only a major theme of the war story and which was oblivious to rather uncomfortable facts.

Central to the Russian account was 'The Great Patriotic War' in which tens of millions of ordinary citizens perished in an act of enormous national sacrifice. It was all too easy to forget the Nazi-Soviet Pact and the subsequent Soviet complicity in the invasion of Poland, the pre war purges which had weakened the Russian military, the lack of preparedness for war in 1941 and the Katyn massacre. The Americans believed they were the 'arsenal of democracy' providing a vast array of men and machines to enable the war to be won. But they conveniently ignored their neutral stance in the first two years of war, which was of little succour to the British. Indeed the limited nature of American help in 1940 became part of the established wartime mythology on both sides of the Atlantic. The French preferred to forget the collaborative association of many people with the Nazis, concentrating instead on the widespread resistance to Nazism. The British wartime myth revolved round the heroics of the Battle of Britain, the miracle of Dunkirk and the nation's stoic defiance during the Blitz. Less attention was given to pre-war appeasement, the lack of emotional restraint in bombing raids and the not inconsiderable crime wave that, in a sense, contradicted the notion of a People's War.

One thing that myths do is to selectively elevate one aspect of reality over another. In all of the above cases, popular memory has elevated the very best of the national wartime record while giving less credible treatment to more embarrassing issues. Those parts of the historical record that set the nation in a positive light are collectively remembered and celebrated. The darker episodes are conveniently sidelined or rather charitably interpreted in a self-serving and biased manner.

Yet this is far from the result of official deception. On the contrary, state sanctioned versions of wartime experience must find some resonance with those who lived through it. To have efficacy, the wartime myth must be shared by the many, not simply propagated by the few. If a mythologised history of a total war resonates with a population, it is because they are party to the myth in question. Here group self-deception may step in.

146

The nation is important in this context because it has been the pre-eminent source of identity in the last two centuries. In the twentieth century, millions of people loyally went to war to defend their nation. Much of this has been owed to the steady inculcation of patriotism by the state. The commitment to the nation and to its institutions can be as important to a person's self-esteem as any purely personal matter. In terms of self-esteem, maintaining one's commitment to a particular view of the nation, in an idealised or heavily mythologised form, can easily involve the same processes of evasion, denial and twisted rationalisation. The whistleblowers who explode national mythologies then become the ultimate iconoclasts of today's liberal societies. It is as if they have violated a sacred, religious code, which has an implicit value for a social group.

In contemporary terms, there are many issues that we would prefer not to think about. We live in an age in which the threats to our security have never been greater. Even after the end of the Cold War, we have enough nuclear weapons to destroy the planet many times over. Nuclear weapons in the wrong hands could be targeted on our cities and our centres of power. Global terrorism certainly remains more potent than ever after the devastation of 9/11. Al Qaeda and their growing band of terrorist supporters constitute a threat to more than 60 countries round their world, and rogue states that possess non-conventional weaponry constitute another unmistakeable danger. Weapons of mass destruction in the wrong hands are part of a nightmarish scenario that we are often reluctant to spell out.

There is every temptation to adopt an 'ostrich mentality' when confronted with seemingly inevitable disaster. Doomsday scenarios are truly unpleasant but wilful inattention will not make them go away. A failure to confront painful facts can sometimes bring us only a Pyrrhic victory.

We cannot afford to abolish all human illusions – that way insanity lies. Yet the demand to seek the truth remains insatiable. Somehow, we must steer between the two if we are to live freely.

Is Folk Psychology Justified?

My entire theory here is based on the assumption that the behaviour of human beings (including self-deceivers) can be explained by folk psychology. Folk psychology is an explanatory and predictive framework in which we attribute a variety of mental states to people to explain and predict their behaviour. These mentalistic states are the propositional attitudes that we attribute in an interpretative manner. They include, but are not exhausted by, states of belief, will, desire, hope and fear. The psychological states that we attribute to an agent to explain his actions will usually, but not always, be those that the agent sees as relevant to performing his actions. They are also the causes of why people act as they do. They are therefore causes of *and* reasons for the agent's behaviour.

In the most basic sense, when we offer a folk-psychological explanation for why Jones goes to the kitchen, we say that Jones has a desire for food, a belief that the food is in the kitchen and then a desire to go to the kitchen to get the food. If we know that Jones wants some food and we can attribute a belief to him that the food is in the kitchen, we can use folk psychology in a predictive manner to say that Jones will go to the kitchen, *ceteris paribus*. Folk psychology has a remarkable capacity for predictive power. The average human is easily able to explain his own and fellow humans' behaviour, and to predict the future course of their actions. As such, it constitutes the most natural and successful strategy any of us can possess for explaining and understanding other people.

Given the presumption of importance attached to this interpretative approach, it is surprising that others should attempt to signal the death of folk psychology. Among those with such a radical approach is Paul Churchland with his brand of eliminative materialism. Eliminative materialism is defined by Churchland as the thesis that folk psychology constitutes a radically false theory, and one whose principles and ontology are in need of displacement. He characterises folk psychology as a stagnating and decadent research program which will eventually be replaced by a mature neuroscience.

Churchland produces a number of specific arguments for rejecting folk psychological explanation. He does not think that the ontology or categories of folk psychology will reduce to neuroscience. He believes instead that we will come to reject folk psychology from our conceptual scheme, in rather the same way that we have rejected folk chemistry, folk physics and folk psychosis. He makes the point that, given the decline of other folk theories, it would be a remarkable thing indeed if folk psychology, whose explanatory domain is much more complex than those of other theories, should be successful. At one point, we had folk theories and concepts to explain heat (via caloric), burning and rusting (via phlogiston), and psychosis (via witchcraft). Each of their theories viewed their respective phenomena through the lens of a specific conceptual scheme and a set of ontological commitments. Then new and better theories emerged which explained the same data with much greater success and simplicity. We found that the older ontology and conceptual scheme was unnecessary and had to be abolished. Thus with the new theory of oxygen propounded by eighteenth-century chemists, there was little need to use the concept of phlogiston to explain rusting. With a highly developed theory of mental illness, witches were deemed to be a pre-scientific part of our world outlook and were similarly abolished. Churchland believes that the lack of adequate match-ups between folk psychological concepts and those of a new powerful neurophysiological theory will yield the same result.

Now, it is true that folk-psychological explanations are unlikely to be reduced to a fully developed neuroscience. In order for one theory to be reduced to another, two things are necessary. Firstly, it is necessary that the reducing theory mirrors the concepts, principles and assumptions of the reduced theory. Secondly, the reducing theory needs a greater success in explaining and predicting the phenomena covered by the (soon to be) reduced theory. Successful reductions have been achieved in this way with the reduction of light to electromagnetic waves, the reduction of sound to compressions of waves and the reduction of heat to kinetic energy.

Davidson, however, has supplied a convincing reason for why folk psychology must remain unreduced and why it ought not to be eliminated. His main reason for advocating the irreducibility of folk psychology is his belief that the predicates of the mental and the physical are unsuited to each other. According to Davidson, the mental and physical are each committed to certain 'constitutive principles' that dictate whether and how we attribute them to agents. They constitute different sources of evidence. Any attempt to reduce mentalistic explanations to those of neuroscience will lead to a mismatch in these constitutive principles. As such, these contrary sets of constitutive principles are a bar to theory reduction.

But what exactly are the characteristics of the mental and physical, such that they are incompatible? Davidson

151

believes that when we attempt to explain an item of behaviour, we are forced to take into account a whole constellation of the agent's motives and beliefs. To do this, we impose what he terms 'conditions of rationality'.

One of the necessary conditions for ascribing beliefs to people is that they possess a large number of interrelated beliefs. If Sarah believes that London is the capital of England, then we presume that she knows what England refers to, what it is for a city to be a capital, and so on. In other words, beliefs as mental states are cross-referenced with a whole host of other mental states that collectively form a network. Stephen Stich describes the case of an elderly lady who has undergone a severe memory loss as a result of a neural disorder. As a young child, she remembered the assassination of President McKinley, but her disorder has caused her to forget everything she once knew about him. She used to know that he was a vice-president who campaigned for various political matters and that he was brutally murdered late in life. However, she now has no concept of assassination or vice-presidency and could not say who McKinley was. Nonetheless, she persistently states that 'McKinley was assassinated'. According to the network criterion outlined above, the senile lady fails to believe that 'McKinley was assassinated', because her understanding of the basic entailments of the belief is impoverished. She lacks a network of related mental states within which a 'belief in the assassination of McKinley' could cohere.

The essence of attributing folk psychological intentional states is that such attributions are guided by purely normative considerations. Normative principles are principles which tell us how things should be. In the case of attributing mental states, they tell us what kinds of belief one should hold and what kinds of actions one should perform on the basis of those beliefs. In this way, mental states, by virtue of their propositional content, help to rationalise or justify other mental states. Our decision not to ascribe the belief to the senile lady that McKinley was assassinated is guided by normative constraints. We decide that there is no interpretative sense in thinking she believes w when she lacks beliefs x, y and z, where x, y and z are necessary entailments of w.

The point Davidson makes is that the condition for the application of mental predicates constitutes a 'source of evidence'. We are at liberty to reject the attribution of a mental state if we find it makes no interpretative sense and leaves us with a radically incoherent agent.

Davidson says that when we attribute a physical state to an agent, we do not take such 'rationality' considerations into account. We can ascribe physical predicates to a person based on certain objective criteria that are not concerned with the 'rationality' conditions of consistency and coherence. All we would need to do is identify that a person was in a verifiable neural state x in order to attribute to him a mental state. There would be little need to identify other physical states before making such an assessment. A simple objective test could reveal the presence of a physical state based on criteria demanded by the physical sciences. Rationality considerations quite simply have no place here. Davidson says that a successful reduction demands that the conditions of attribution would have to be the same with physical and mental states; however, this is not going to be the case.

If we accept that whenever a mental state is attributed to a subject, necessarily a physical attribute must be also, then mental states will, according to Davidson, lose allegiance to their proper source of evidence. We would not want to ascribe to the elderly lady a belief in McKinley's assassination on the basis of a physical analysis of her brain state, but this is the implication of Churchland's argument. This set of arguments shows that any attempt to reduce folk-psychological explanations to those of any physical science will leave us with a radically deficient explanation of human behaviour. Instead, as Davidson makes clear, we should regard the process of mentalistic attribution as having a level of *autonomous irreducibility*.

Churchland criticises folk psychology on other grounds. He writes that the content and the success of folk psychology have barely advanced in nearly three thousand years, something that to his mind reflects its essential stagnation and infertility. According to Churchland, the folk psychology used by the Greeks is essentially the same theory as the one we employ today, and, for Churchland, we are negligibly better at explaining human behaviour in its terms than was Sophocles.

Even if we accept that belief-desire psychology has changed little over two millennia, this does not constitute a reason to discard the theory. The plays of Sophocles and Euripides are exceptionally popular today and are still regularly performed. This owes something to the fact that their analyses of human behaviour strike a chord with modern audiences who recognise familiar patterns of human behaviour. Even though ancient and modern settings are dissimilar, the plays deal with the same categories of behaviour and utilise familiar interpersonal situations. As Strawson puts it, '... there is a massive central core of human thinking which has no history ... there are categories and concepts which ... change not at all'. The penetrating ancient analyses of human behaviour made by the Greeks seem to be very close to those of modernity. Given this, we ought to conclude that the concepts of folk psychology constitute a perennially successful method for explaining and predicting human behaviour.

Another reason for maintaining folk psychology is concerned with the concept of 'multiple realisability'. If

154

we were to try to produce lengthy and complicated predictions of behaviour solely employing a stock of concepts from neural science, I do not think we would actually understand the basis of behaviour. This is because an analysis of behaviour reveals discernible patterns which could not be captured in purely physical descriptions.

In his article 'True Believers', Dennett outlines an interesting thought experiment. Imagine, he says, that a Martian race of vastly superior intelligence were to descend upon earth to watch our behaviour. They are all superphysicists, capable of comprehending all activity at a purely micro level. They visit Wall Street and instead of seeing buildings, brokers and bids, they tune in to their microperceptual level and observe vast congeries of subatomic particles milling about. Being such good physicists, they predict that at a certain moment the following day, a stockbroker will telephone his colleague and ask him to pass on a message to sell a well-known commodity. Sure enough, the event takes place.

When they trace the causal ancestry of the events that led to the stockbroker's phone call, they observe a long chain of physical events that they believe tells an adequate explanatory story. The causal explanation, however, fails to capture the way in which the same behaviour could have been brought about in a number of other ways, all underlined by a different set of physical events. The stockbroker could have made the call in many different ways using different series of finger motions. He could have spoken louder or softer (thereby implying differences in vocal-cord vibrations) and achieved an identical effect. In the thought experiment, if events suddenly took a turn for the worse and the building had to be evacuated, the stockbroker could have made the call from outside the building or at home.

The same effect and the same item of behaviour (making

155

a phone call) could be produced if the micro-level events were different. This is because there will be a redundancy of fallback mechanisms to ensure the desired effect is brought about. The fallback mechanisms are directly related to the fact that there is usually more than one way to bring about a desired effect. If I want to make a phone call, circumstances in the physical world will usually allow me to do this in a vast number of ways. In a reductive analysis using the purely underlying physical events, the causal explanations do not consider this causal resiliency. Their causal explanations tie an explanation down to a specific cause and do not take into account what could have been otherwise.

What they fail to see from the physical stance, but what we can see from our intentional stance, is that intentional states and behaviour (i.e. making phone calls) are multiply realisable and can be brought about at a micro level via a number of patterns of physical events. To put it differently, causality can be said to have a certain 'resiliency'. When someone wants to bring something about and an initial method is frustrated, another may be employed. If plan a fails, plan b is attempted. Plan b might reflect an identical goal, but this will be realised in a different physical manner. If we concentrate merely on the one way in which something is brought about, we fail to appreciate the many alternative ways in which the same physical result could have been achieved. Concentrating purely on the micro level events does not reveal the open-ended capability of the intentional mind. For these reasons, at least, it is premature to announce the death of folk psychology. The theory is certainly here to stay.

Appendix 2

A Favoured Belief Which is Rational

The model I have proposed for understanding self-deception rests on various assumptions about our relationship with unfavourable evidence and the beliefs it gives rise to. I argued that in self-deception an agent first encounters and accepts the import of evidence supporting a given proposition. This leads to a belief in that proposition which the agent finds somewhat unwelcome, thus leading to a desire to believe the opposite belief. Self-deception then involves the promotion of a favourable belief that is held in the teeth of contradictory evidence and which is less psychologically disturbing for the agent. The rational, evidentially supported belief is buried and the irrational and non-evidentially supported belief is promoted. This model for understanding self-deception makes one assumption that could be questioned. Self-deception arguably need not involve a promoted belief that it is irrational to hold. I will outline this with an example.

Geoff is a successful accountant who works for a large and successful accountancy firm. He has been happily employed for over two years and there is every sign of rapid promotion and pay increases. There are no signs that the company will dispense with staff; indeed they are happy to employ new staff as part of a global expansion. In spite of the bright future that the company promises,

Geoff begins to worry incessantly about becoming unemployed. Though there is no evidence of impending company problems, Geoff constantly questions his work colleagues about the likelihood of becoming unemployed. Though they remind him that his fears are groundless, it is clear from certain private moments that his fears will not go away. He constantly scans local newspapers for other jobs and phones the employment-counselling service.

When his peers suggest that he really does believe in the imminent collapse of the company, he goes into denial and insists that he thinks no such thing. Clearly here, the belief that is unfavourable, namely that 'I will lose my job and become unemployed', is causing him considerable anxiety. It motivates him to promote a favoured belief, namely that 'I will stay on at this successful company.' His promoted belief, unlike the other core cases, is very much based on the available evidence and is perfectly rational. The evidence directly contradicts the unfavoured belief and he should have no reason for concern.

I think we can all find this example entirely familiar from everyday life even if it differs from the standard cases of self-deception found in philosophical textbooks. It need not contradict the foregoing analysis however. For we can surely be self-deceived about our own thinking processes, irrespective of whether we are thinking about a topic in rational or irrational ways. Normal analyses of self-deception start with people accepting evidence about the world which rationally leads to an unfavoured belief. This worldly belief can be about their own behaviour, their abilities or the behaviour of friends.

If one becomes self-deceived about one's thoughts, however, the case is slightly different. Geoff ought to accept that the evidence from his own moods and behaviour is 'I believe I will be fired.' This anxiety-provoking rogue belief needs to be self-deceptively repudiated, and he

158

therefore adopts techniques for making himself think that he believes the opposite. Geoff becomes self-deceived about his thinking processes by misinterpreting or distorting evidence about what he *thinks* about his job, not by misinterpreting or distorting evidence about his job. This may seem an unlikely analysis, but it enables the conditions outlined to cover far more cases of self-deception than other similar analyses.

Notes

1 All quotes from *The Irving Judgement* pp. 298–347.
2 For an excellent discussion of the Irving trial read *The Holocaust on Trial* by D.D. Gutterplan.
3 Michael Martin, 'Introduction' in *Self-deception and Self-understanding*, ed. M. Martin (University Press of Kansas, Kansas, 1985), p. 1.
4 David Nyberg, *The Varnished Truth* (The University of Chicago Press, Chicago), p. 87.
5 ibid. p. 88.
6 Frederick Schmitt, 'Epistemic Dimensions of Self-deception' in *Perspectives on Self-deception*, ed. Brian McLaughlin and Amelie Rorty (University of California Press, California, 1985), p. 195.
7 For more on this see David Nyberg, *The Varnished Truth* (The University of Chicago Press, Chicago), Chapter 4.
8 Here doxastic refers to 'belief'. A doxastic disparity is a disparity between beliefs.
9 Marcia Cavell, *The Psychoanalytic Mind* (Harvard University Press, 1996), p. 194.
10 It should be stressed that we are dealing here (as with self-deception) with paradigm or core examples of other deception. Annette Barnes lists a number of variants to the familiar type of this deception, including

160

the conceptual possibility of x deceiving y into believing the truth, and x deceiving y into believing what x takes to be true. I contend that these cases are plausible but atypical.

11 Alfred Mele, 'Real Self-deception' in *Behaviour and Brain Sciences*, March 1997, p. 99.
12 Robert Audi, 'Self-deception, Rationalization and Reasons for Acting' in *Perspectives on Self-deception*, ed. Brian McLaughlin and Amelie Rorty (University of California Press, California, 1985), p. 94.
13 J. Canfield and D. Gustafson, 'Self-deception', *Analysis* 23 (1962), p. 35.
14 Patrick Gardiner, *Proceedings of the Aristotelian Society* 70 (1969–70): 244.
15 A Mele, 'Real Self-deception' in *Behaviour and Brain Sciences*, March 1997, p. 91.
16 ibid. p. 95.
17 Alfred Mele, *Irrationality* (Oxford University Press, Oxford, 1987), pp. 125–6.
18 Alfred Mele, 'Real Self-deception' in *Behaviour and Brain Sciences* (March 1997), p. 94.
19 ibid. p. 95.
20 Propositional attitudes are ascriptions of mental states held by an individual which are about something in the world – 'John believes that the cat is on the mat'.
21 Sebastian Gardner, *Irrationality and the Philosophy of Psychoanalysis* (Cambridge University Press, Cambridge, 1993), p. 60.
22 David Pears, *Motivated Irrationality* (Oxford University Press, Oxford, 1984), p. 86.
23 David Pears, 'Goals and Strategies of Self-deception' in *The Multiple Self*, ed. J Elster (Cambridge University Press, Cambridge, 1985), p. 71.
24 David Pears, *Motivated Irrationality*, p. 87.
25 ibid. p. 91.

26 ibid. p. 91.
27 Sebastian Gardner, *Irrationality and the Philosophy of Psychoanalysis* (Cambridge University Press, Cambridge, 1993), p. 76.
28 ibid. p. 81.
29 Alfred Mele, 'Real Self-deception' in *Behaviour and Brain Sciences* (March 1997) p. 93.
30 Mark Johnston 'Self-deception and the nature of the mind', in *Perspectives on Self-deception*, eds Brian McLaughlin and Amelie Rorty (University of California Press, California, 1985), p. 66.
31 ibid. p. 65.
32 ibid. p. 65.
33 ibid. p. 70.
34 ibid. p. 72.
35 ibid. p. 75.
36 ibid. p. 76.
37 D. Gilbert and J. Cooper, 'Social-Psychological Strategies of Self-deception', in *Self-deception and Self-understanding*, ed. M. Martin (University Press of Kansas, Kansas, 1985), p. 78.
38 ibid. p. 79.
39 Ziva Kunda, 'The Case for Motivated Reasoning' in *Psychological Bulletin* 108, p. 483.
40 Ziva Kunda, 'Motivated Inference: self-serving generation and evaluation of causal theories' in *Journal of Personality and Social Psychology* 53, p. 644.
41 R. Nisbett and L. Ross, *Human Inference* (Prentice Hall, NJ, 1980) p. 12.
42 ibid. p. 44.
43 ibid. p. 47.
44 ibid. p. 45.
45 ibid. p. 46.
46 ibid. p. 18.
47 ibid. p. 186.

48 ibid. p. 179.
49 ibid. p. 180.
50 ibid. p. 181.
51 ibid. p. 180.
52 Annette Barnes, *Seeing Through Self-deception* (Cambridge University Press, Cambridge, 1997), p. 96.
53 Donald Davidson, 'Deception and division', p. 138.
54 Donald Davidson 'Paradoxes of Irrationality' in *Philosophical Essays on Freud*, ed. by J. Hopkins and R. Wollheim (Cambridge University Press, Cambridge, 1982), p. 304.
55 ibid. p. 301.
56 ibid. p. 304.
57 I do not go as far as thinking that partitions are always characterised by segregated intentional structures, as there are cases of self-deception involving only segregated contrary beliefs (i.e. cases of unintentional self-deception).
58 John Heil, 'Minds Divided', *Mind*, 98, 1989, p. 575.
59 Donald Davidson, 'Paradoxes of Irrationality' in *Philosophical Essays on Freud*, ed. by J. Hopkins and R. Wollheim (Cambridge University Press, Cambridge, 1982), p. 304.
60 Marcia Cavell, *The Psychoanalytic Mind* (Harvard University Press, Cambridge, Mass, 1993), p. 201.
61 Stuart Hampshire, *Thought and Action* (Chatto & Windus, London, 1966), p. 119.
62 Annette Barnes, *Seeing Through Self-deception* (Cambridge University Press, Cambridge, 1997), p. 92.
63 Bruce Wiltshire, 'Mimetic Engulfment' in *Perspectives on Self-deception*, eds Brian McLaughlin and Amelie Rorty (University of California Press, California, 1985), pp. 392–3.
64 Mark Johnston, 'Self-deception and the Nature of the Mind' in *Perspectives on Self-deception*, eds Brian

McLaughlin and Amelie Rorty (University of California Press, California, 1985), p. 87.

65 ibid. p. 88.
66 ibid. p. 87.
67 Marcia Cavell, *The Psychoanalytic Mind* (Harvard University Press, Cambridge, Mass, 1993), p. 200.
68 Sigmund Freud (1915e), p. 169.
69 Sigmund Freud (1912g), pp. 51–2.
70 Sigmund Freud (1925d), p. 215.
71 Sigmund Freud (1915e), p. 171.
72 ibid. p. 170.
73 Sigmund Freud (1915e), p. 172.
74 Sigmund Freud (1915e), p. 191.
75 ibid. p. 172.
76 Sigmund Freud (1915d), p. 147.
77 Sigmund Freud (1916–17), pp. 327–9.
78 Sigmund Freud (1926d), p. 242.
79 In Freud's later theory, anxiety plays a crucial part in both causing and being a by-product of repression. In *Inhibitions, Symptoms and Anxiety*, Freud developed a signal theory of anxiety whereby the ego is hypothesised to emit a signal of displeasure when it encounters an unwanted instinctual impulse from the id. Repression is seen as the attempt to block out anxiety by blocking out awareness of the thoughts or impulses occasioning it. Symptoms, therefore, are only formed in order to avoid anxiety.
80 Sigmund Freud (1926e), p. 304.
81 Sigmund Freud (1923a), p. 153.
82 These include obsessive-compulsive disorder, hysterical illness, neurotic depression, hypersensitive paranoia and a range of states of anxiety.
83 Sigmund Freud (1916–17), p. 297.
84 Sigmund Freud (1909d), p. 48.
85 ibid. p. 47.

86 ibid. p. 60.
87 ibid. p. 85.
88 Sigmund Freud (1916–17), p. 302.
89 Hopkins illustrates this point by discussing the hypothetical case of a man whose action of lunging at lampposts is described in terms of his possession of an Oedipal desire (represented symbolically) to kill his father.
90 Jean-Paul Sartre, *Being and Nothingness* (Hazel Barnes, London, 1958), pp. 51–3.
91 ibid. pp. 51–3.
92 ibid. pp. 53–4.
93 Sigmund Freud (1940a), pp. 439–40.
94 Donald Davidson, 'Paradoxes of Irrationality', in *Philosophical Essays on Freud*, eds James Hopkins and Richard Wollheim (Cambridge University Press, Cambridge, 1982), p. 304.
95 Robert Trivers, 'Introduction' in Richard Dawkins, *The Selfish Gene* (Oxford University Press, Oxford, 1976).
96 Walter Laqueur, The Terrible Secret (Penguin, Harmondsworth, 1981), p. 207.
97 Ibid. p. 205.
98 Ibid. p. 199.
99 Ibid. p. 206.
100 Danish politicians had come to hear of the plan and then tipped off the Chief Rabbi who, in turn, advised the Jewish population to hide until transport to Sweden could be arranged. Aided by a largely sympathetic population, nearly 90% of Danish Jews escaped to Sweden as a result of this tip off.

Bibliography – Main works consulted

Audi, Robert, 'Self-deception and Rationality' in *Self-deception and Self-understanding*, ed. by Mike Martin (University Press of Kansas, Lawrence, 1985).

Audi, Robert, 'Self-deception, Rationalisation, and Reasons for Acting' in *Perspectives on Self-deception*, ed. by B. McLaughlin and A. Rorty (University of California Press, California, 1988).

Barnes, Annette, *Seeing Through Self-deception* (Cambridge University Press, Cambridge, 1997).

Baron, Marcia, 'What is Wrong with Self-deception' in *Perspectives on Self-deception*, ed. by B. McLaughlin and A. Rorty (University of California Press, California, 1988).

Cavell, Marcia, *The Psychoanalytic Mind* (Harvard University Press, Cambridge, Mass, 1993).

Clark, David S., *What Freud Really Said* (London: Pelican, 1967).

Davidson, Donald, 'Mental Events' in *Essays on Actions and Events* (Cambridge University Press, Cambridge, 1980).

Davidson, Donald, 'Deception and Division' in *Actions and Events*, ed. by E. LePore and B. McLaughlin (Basil Blackwell, New York, 1985).

Davidson, Donald, 'Paradoxes of Irrationality' in

Philosophical Essays on Freud, ed. by James Hopkins and Richard Wollheim (Cambridge University Press, Cambridge, 1982).

Demos, Raphael, 'Lying to Oneself', *Journal of Philosophy* 57 (1960), pp. 588–95.

Dilman, I., *Freud and the Mind* (Blackwell Publishers, Oxford, 1984).

Elster, John, *Sour Grapes* (Cambridge University Press, Cambridge, 1983).

Elster, John (ed.), *The Multiple Self* (Cambridge University Press, Cambridge, 1985).

Erwin, Edward, 'Psychoanalysis and Self-deception' in *Perspectives on Self-deception*, ed. by B. McLaughlin and A. Rorty (University of California Press, California, 1988).

Fingarette, Herbert, *Self-deception* (Routledge and Kegan Paul, London, 1969).

Freud, Sigmund, *The Interpretation of Dreams* (1900a) in PFL vol. 4.

Freud, Sigmund, 'An Analysis of a Case of Phobia in a Five-Year-Old Boy' (1909d) in PFL vol. 9.

Freud, Sigmund, 'Repression' (1915d) in PFL vol. 11.

Freud, Sigmund, *The Unconscious* (1915e) in PFL vol. 11.

Freud, Sigmund, *Introductory Lectures on Psychoanalysis* (1916–17) PFL vol. 1.

Freud, Sigmund, 'Two Encyclopaedia Articles' (1923a) in PFL vol. 15.

Freud, Sigmund, *A Short Account of Psychoanalysis* (1924f) in PFL vol. 15.

Freud, Sigmund, *An Autobiographical Study* (1925d) in PFL vol. 15.

Freud, Sigmund, *Inhibitions, Symptoms and Anxiety* (1926d) in PFL vol. 10.

Freud, Sigmund, 'The Question of Lay Analysis' (1926e) in PFL vol. 15.

167

Freud, Sigmund, *New Introductory Lectures on Psychoanalysis* (1933a) in PFL vol. 2.

Gardner, Sebastian, *Irrationality and the Philosophy of Psychoanalysis* (Cambridge University Press, Cambridge, 1993).

Gergen, Kenneth, 'The Ethnopsychology of Self-deception' in *Self-deception and Self-understanding*, ed. by Mike Martin (University Press of Kansas, Lawrence, 1985).

Glover, Jonathan, *I: The Philosophy and Psychology of Personal Identity* (Pelican, London, 1988).

Guttenplan, Samuel (ed.), *Companion to the Philosophy of Mind* (Blackwell Publishers, Cambridge, 1993).

Hopkins, James, 'Introduction' to *Philosophical Essays on Freud*, ed. by James Hopkins and Richard Wollheim (Cambridge University Press, Cambridge, 1982).

Johnston, Mark, 'Self-deception and the Nature of the Mind' in *Perspectives on Self-deception*, ed. by B. McLaughlin and A. Rorty (University of California Press, California, 1988).

McLaughlin, Brian, 'Exploring the possibility of Self-deception in Belief' in *Perspectives on Self-deception*, ed. by B. McLaughlin and A. Rorty (University of California Press, California, 1988).

Martin, Mike, 'Introduction', *Self-deception and Self-understanding*, ed. by Mike Martin (University Press of Kansas, Lawrence, 1985).

Mele, Alfred, *Irrationality: An Essay on Akrasia, Self-deception, and Self-control* (Oxford University Press, Oxford, 1987).

Mele, Alfred, 'Real Self-deception' in *Behavioural and Brain Sciences*, March 1997, pp. 91–102.

Neu, J. (ed.), *Cambridge Companion to Freud* (Cambridge University Press, Cambridge, 1991).

Nisbet, R. and Ross, L., *Human Inference: Strategies and*

Shortcomings of Social Judgement (Prentice Hall, NJ, 1980).

Nyberg, David, *The Varnished Truth* (The University of Chicago Press, Chicago, 1993).

Pears, David, *Motivated Irrationality* (Oxford University Press, Oxford, 1984).

Pears, David, 'Goals and Strategies of Self-deception' in *The Multiple Self*, ed. by Jon Elster. (Cambridge University Press, Cambridge, 1985).

Rorty, Amelie, 'The Deceptive Self: liars, layers and lairs' in *Perspectives on Self-deception*, ed. by B. McLaughlin and A. Rorty (University of California Press, London, 1988).

Rycroft, Charles, *Psychoanalysis Observed* (Pelican, London, 1968).

Sandford, David, 'Self-deception as Rationalisation' in *Perspectives on Self-deception*, ed. by B. McLaughlin and A. Rorty (University of California Press, California, 1988).

Sartre, Jean-Paul, *Being and Nothingness* (Washington Square Press, 1966).

Schmitt, Frederick, 'Epistemic Dimensions of Self-deception' in *Perspectives on Self-deception*, ed. by B. McLaughlin and A. Rorty (University of California Press, California, 1988).

Storr, Anthony, *Freud* (Oxford University Press, Oxford, 1989).

Sutherland, Stuart, *Irrationality: The Enemy Within* (Pelican, London, 1992).

Szabados, Béla, 'Self-deception', *Canadian Journal of Philosophy*, vol. 4, no. 1 (1974), pp. 51–68.

Szabados, Béla, 'The Self, Its Passions and Self-deception' in *Self-deception and Self-understanding*, ed. by Mike Martin (University Press of Kansas, Lawrence, 1985).

Talbott, William, 'Intentional Self-deception in a Single

Coherent Self', *Philosophy and Phenomenological Research*, vol. 55, no. 1 (March 1995), pp. 27–74.

Wiltshire, Bruce, 'Mimetic Engulfment' in *Perspectives on Self-deception*, ed. by B. McLaughlin and A. Rorty (University of California Press, California, 1988).

Wollheim, Richard, *Freud* (Fontana, London, 1971).

The standard reference for all Freudian primary literature is the 24-volume Standard Edition (ed. J. Strachey). However I have made use of the 15-volume Pelican Freud Library (PFL). All references are from this edition of Freud's writings. See the bibliography for more details.

170